HINDI MORPHOLOGY
A Word-based Description

MLBD SERIES IN LINGUISTICS

General Editor
DHANESH JAIN

Volume IX

HINDI MORPHOLOGY
A Word-based Description

By

Rajendra Singh
Rama Kant Agnihotri

MOTILAL BANARSIDASS PUBLISHERS
PRIVATE LIMITED • DELHI

First Edition: Delhi, 1997

ISBN: 81-208-1446-0

Also available at:

MOTILAL BANARSIDASS
41 U.A. Bungalow Road, Jawahar Nagar, Delhi 110 007
8 Mahalaxmi Chamber, Warden Road, Mumbai 400 026
120 Royapettah High Road, Mylapore, Chennai 600 004
Sanas Plaza, Subhash Nagar, Pune 411 002
16 St. Mark's Road, Bangalore 560 001
8 Camac Street, Calcutta 700 017
Ashok Rajpath, Patna 800 004
Chowk, Varanasi 221 001

PRINTED IN INDIA
BY JAINENDRA PRAKASH JAIN AT SHRI JAINENDRA PRESS,
A-45 NARAINA, PHASE I, NEW DELHI 110 028
AND PUBLISHED BY NARENDRA PRAKASH JAIN FOR
MOTILAL BANARSIDASS PUBLISHERS PRIVATE LIMITED,
BUNGALOW ROAD, DELHI 110 007

Dedicated to

MURARI LAL UPRETI,

SUDESH, SAROJ

and

UMESH

CONTENTS

ABBREVIATIONS

abs	abstract
adj	adjective
adv	adverb
ani	animate
aux	auxiliary
C	consonant
caus	causative
comp	comparative
contin	contingent
dimi	diminutive
fem	feminine
fut	future
h	honorific
hum	human
inani	inanimate
inf	infinitive
imper	imperative
imperf	imperfect
inten	intensive
intrans	intransitive
masc	masculine
n	noun
neg	negative
nom	nomative
nh	non-honorific
obl	oblique
ono	onomatopoeic
opt	optative
part adj	participial adjective
perf	perfect
pl	plural
poss	possessive
pp	past participle
pres p	present participle

pres t	present tense
pt	past tense
sing	singular
trans	transitive
V	vowel
v	verb
vi	verb intransitive
voc	vocative
vt	verb transitive
I	first person
II	second person (*tum* 'you')
II (nh)	second person (non-honorific *tu* 'you')
II (h)	second (honorific *ap* 'you')
III	third person

A Note on the Transcription Systems

Largely following Ohala (1983). IPA symbols have been used to transcribe data from Modern Hindi. Widely accepted standard Roman transcription system has been followed to transcribe Hindi and Sanskrit technical terms.

Examples of Hindi data:

दूधवाला	dudhvala	'milkman'
कहानी	kɔhani	'story'
कहानियाँ	kəhanɪy̯ã	'stories'
लूट	luʈ	'loot'

Examples of Hindi and Sanskrit technical terms:

द्विकर्मक	dvikarmak	'ditransitive'
धातु	dhātu	'root'
व्युतपन्न प्रातिपदिक	vyutpann prātipadik	'derived nominals'

PREFACE

This book is our way of saying 'thank you' to Modern Hindi, a language that has nourished and enriched certain aspects of our lives. In presenting a very full description of the morphology of Hindi, we have tried to make sense of the relevant facts of the matter *with* (and not *for*) the speakers of Hindi.

Although we began talking about morphology and Hindi morphology in 1990, when the second author was a Shastri Fellow in Montreal, the book began in earnest in 1992. Hundreds of letters, conversations, faxes, and telephone calls later, we are pleased to put it on public display. Precisely what our labour of love adds up to, we shall leave for the community of scholars (of Hindi, in particular) to decide.

We are grateful to Dr. Gautam Sengupta for repeatedly drawing our attention to matters of economy and elegance and Dr. Alan Ford for sharing our enthusiasm for the description that constiutes this book and for contributing to it anonymously. We are also grateful to Profs. P. Dasgupta, W. Dressler, Paul Kiparksy, K.P. Mohanan, Y.C. Morin, P. Muysken, Prem Singh, A.K. Sinha and K.V. Subbarao for several useful discussions that have indirectly contributed much to this book. Thanks are due to Mr. U.S. Bahri for producing the camera-ready copy of this book.

Montreal
Delhi
August 1996

Rajendra Singh
Rama Kant Agnihotri

CHAPTER 1

INTRODUCTION

1.0 *Preliminaries*

The purpose of this book is to provide a full, hopefully exhaustive, description of the morphology of Modern Hindi (MH). Although the discussion of how full the description we will provide turns out to be can, and perhaps must, be left to others, we must clarify the other terms used in the statement of our objectives: *description, morphology,* and *Modern Hindi*. None of these terms can be taken for granted. Nor can the crucial term in the sub-title of the book: *word-based*.

Description is normally used in an a-theoretical way, an indication of the empiricist bias of modern social science with its emphasis on what it calls 'facts'. Very often, it is merely an old theory, a new theory has not been able to accommodate.

We shall, however, refrain from participating here in the debate summarized above, and admit quite frankly that the description to be provided is guided by the theory outlined in Chapter 3 and motivated, for MH, in Chapter 4. Although we believe the description we shall provide to be the only possible adequate description, we shall leave the ultimate validity of that belief to the judgement of the community of MH scholars.

Morphology is no less tricky than *description*. We take it to mean that part of lexical relatedness which satisfies the joint requirements of formal and semantic similarity. In this view of morphology, the relation that exists between *good* and *bad*, the relation of antonymy, is not a matter of morphology; nor is the relationship between the past-tense of *read* and the colour adjective *red*.

Lexical relatedness, if construed as a domain of rational enquiry, is vast, and must encompass ethnology, ethnography, psychoanalysis, pattern-recognition, and several other things, including the culturally sanctioned order of the alphabet or the syllabury, the order used by lexicography to capture some of lexical relatedness. We are, it is important to point out, concerned with only a very small, though hopefully central, part of this vast domain.

There are, obviously, various ways of talking about what we refer to as morphology here. We shall outline and motivate our way of talking about it in Chapters 3 and 4. Here it is sufficient to point out that what we are calling morphology has to do with the lexical relatedness that can be legitimately said to exist between pairs of words like *luṭ* 'rob' and *luṭ* 'loot', *dudh* 'milk' and *dudhvala* 'milkman', *kəhani* 'story' and *kəhanıyā̃* 'stories', and *məst* 'carefree' and *məsti* 'carefreeness'.

The sort of lexical relatedness examplified above can be said to be constitutive of the MH speaker's knowledge of his language. A description of that knowledge is not necessarily a representation of that knowledge. The latter must meet several additional criteria contemporary psycholinguistics has attempted to develop. Although we shall, in Chapters 9 and 10, attempt to take a few steps in the direction of transforming our description into a possible representation, we shall, in general, be making the weak, descriptive claim. Hence the word *description* in the opening sentence of this introduction.

We should also point out that although morphology must, and generally does, include the formation of compound words from simple words, we shall not provide a description of compound formation in MH in this book. Another book-length description will be needed for that, and hopefully we will get to it one of these days. Since partial and complete reduplication in MH (cf. Singh 1985) can be said to operate with a single word input and a two-word word output, we have also excluded reduplicative word-formation processes from this study. Both exclusions are only practical decisions, and carry no theoretical import. We also exclude from consideration word-formation techniques and processes that, though very useful and productive in fulfilling the neologistic needs of MH, do not belong to morphology: acronyms, clippings, and other methods that do not meet the joint criteria of formal and semantic relatedness (cf. Dressler and Barbaresi 1994). The difference between the first two exclusions and the third one resides in the fact that whereas the first two could have been included, the last one is not morphology to begin with. We regret excluding compounding and reduplication, but have nothing to say about acronyms, clippings and their congeners.

Modern Hindi, like 'English','German', or 'French' are, as anthropologists, ethnographers and sociologists will tell us any day of the week, highly problematic terms. They raise a number of issues, and we cannot even list the ones we shall not be able to take up here (cf. Urciuoli 1991; Mey 1990 etc.). We shall, instead, only describe the operational heuristic we have used to delimit what we mean by MH, and outline what we believe is a reasonable external history of it.

Although there are a considerable number of cobwebs to be removed from labels such as 'Hindi', 'Hindustani', 'Urdu', 'Modern Standard

Hindi'(MSH), one must begin with the observation that the language we seek to describe a part of can be said to have as many as six hundred million speakers (Bhatia 1987:9). Contemporary glotto-political currents may change the picture substantially in the years to come, but, till recently, there has been a *social* consensus that these six hundred million speakers share the same language, a consensus not very different from the one that allows one to refer to Quebecoise or Quebec French and to 'Merican' as American English. It is socio-politic in nature, but it has clearly been there.

For a large proportion of the six hundred million mentioned above MSH is only "a second or third speech style" (Gumperz and Naim 1969). There is, however, a sizeable number of speakers, mostly third or fourth generation unbanites, who can legitimately claim MSH as their "native language" (cf. Ohala 1983 also). We shall see below how and why some of this has come about.

The academic folk-lore about Hindi goes as follows. *Hindi* is the modern name for *Hindui*, *Hindavi*, *Rexti*, a mixed speech spoken around Delhi. It was established as a *lingua franca* between the natives of the area and Arabs, Afghans, Persians, and Turks during the 13th century. Because it was used with and by soldiers camping in and around Delhi during the consolidation of Moghul power, it was given the alternate name *Urdu*, a Turkish word meaning camp.

The non-academic folk-lore construes Hindi and Urdu as two different languages, which is what they have become except for the linguist. In this folk-lore, Hindus speak Hindi and Muslims speak Urdu, though what they speak may be the same. Some cross-over is recognized and acknowledged.

Hindi is, thus, in a real sense the *enfant terrible* of modern linguistics, defying several of its dichotomies. To understand some of the category-defying behaviour of this *enfant*, we need to embed our discussion in a larger matrix. We shall begin with the outline of the general picture, and then get down to disentangling some specific knots.

1.1 *The Development of Modern Hindi*

MH is generally assumed to have developed from Old Indo-Aryan (OIA) or Vedic Sanskrit through the intermediate stages of Classical Sanskrit, the Pali-Prakrits, and Apabhransha. The specific route this development took is not yet fully agreed upon by scholars. The general consensus is that it is a direct descendant of Sauraseni Prakrit via Apabhransha. Vajpeyi (1958: 5-14), however, postulates another Prakrit as its source, *Kaurwi*, and designates the Apbhransha of this hypothetical Prakrit as the immediate source of this New Indo-Aryan (NIA) language.

As far as the date of its origin is concerned, most scholars prefer the 11th century. The earlist date suggested is 9th century, and Vajpeyi provides some evidence for that suggestion. But even he would agree that the consolidation, such as it was, takes place a bit later. Amrit Rai (1984: 55 and elsewhere) argues that it coincides with Ghazni setting up his capital in Lahore in 1027. Guru (1920:13) is a bit more conservative and prefers the 12th century. The disagreement, it should be obvious, is minimal, particularly for a question as complex as this.

The region of North-India over which the immediate ancestor of MH could be said to have been distributed, would, obviously, vary according to what that ancestor is assumed to have been.

Vajpeyi restricts it to what he calls *Kurujanpad*, which, according to him, extended from (modern) Muradabad in Uttar Pradesh to Ambala in Haryana and included the modern towns of Muzaffarnagar, Saharanpur, Meerut, and Dehradun in Uttar Pradesh. Rai, however, persuasively argues that Hindavi was the literary language of northern India at the time when Muslims appeared on the scene. It was a composite literary language in its very formative years, and received new influences with the same vigour with which it had synthesized elements from Haryanavi, Eastern Punjabi, Rajasthani, and Braj. The new dialectal differentiation leads to other separate languages.

Although further precision is needed in the brief historical outline provided above, what is needed most for a synchronic description is some help in disentangling what might be called the Hindi/Urdu problem. That help is avilable in Rai. He argues, very convincingly indeed, that they both come from the same source and that the division of Hindi and Urdu is a slow, deliberate political act.

Apparently, the decline of the Moghul empire inspired some elites to hold steadfastly on to what they considered to be the most visible symbol of their superiority and prowess. The Iranianization of Hindavi is a result of the effort by those elites. Their reformist zeal led to the purification of Hindavi and the consequent establishment of Urdu. The fault line created by these elites on the run was fully, if not deliberately, exploited by the British. Amir Khusro's Punjabi-Haryanavi-Rajasthani-Khari Boli-Braj patois of Delhi is transformed into Urdu or Zaban-e-Dehlavi during the reign of Aurangzeb. This reformist adventure that accomplished this transformation was even codified by Shah Hatim in his *Divanzada* (1755). The edicts, as presented by Rai (1984:249), read as follows:

1. (Use of such words from) the Arabic and Persian languages as are near to comprehension and widely used.
2. Words of all other languages, including Hindavi words, which they call 'bhaka', are to be discarded.
3. Only those words of common everyday usage are acceptable which the elite approve of.
4. The usages of Delhi, which are the idiom of the Mirazas (i.e. the Royality) of India and the pleasure-seeking men of culture, are to be accepted.
5. Restore their original spellings to Arabic and Persian words....

A reaction was inevitable, and it took the form of a movement to High Hindi, which, as Ohala attests, has produced the possibility of acquiring Hindi as a native language . What Gandhi called Hindustani, and which is what *we* mean by Hindi, was the complement language of the generations preceding those mentioned by Ohala. The complementarity was and to a large extent still is such that Hindi and Urdu could have been and in fact were (cf. Kelkar 1968; Cardona 1974:439; Khubchandani 1978:4, amongst others) analyzed as institutionalized stylistic variants. They may have however, changed for ever. Although that possibility remains a real one for a large number of speakers, what is also pertinent is the fact that High Hindi now really has, to twist the traditional linguistic metaphor, acquired some native speakers. The recent constitutionalization of Urdu as a separate language will, obviously, do the same thing for the hitherto 'other style'. We shall, however, concentrate on the common core, on what Kelkar (1968) appropriately calls 'Hirdu'. That is what we mean by Hindi, and this book is an attempt to deal with a small part of the linguistic competence of urban, educated MH speakers.

1.2 *A Word-based Description*

Word-based, the last term for which we must provide a preliminary explanation here, is the most difficult of all since it raises Aristotle's paradox. Although its full meaning will become clear only after the reader has worked his way through Chapters 4 and 8, few somewhat pre-emptive preliminary remarks may not be entirely out of order. The sense we intend to convey is that there are alternative ways of looking at morphology and that we prefer, for reasons sketched out in Chapter 4, to take word as the basic unit of morphology. The other, in fact the standard, alternative takes what it calls the morpheme as the basic unit. Whereas the point of view taken here is related to the one presumably the *padvadins* defended (cf. Matilal 1985), the standard view is quintessentially Pāṇinian. Whereas the Western avatars of Pāṇini include Bloomfield, Hockett, Halle, and Kiparsky, the Western padvadins include Varon, Kuyrolowicz, and, to a certain extent, Vennemann and Jackendoff. Our intention is to exploit this almost lost or forgotten tradition, but it is guided not by nostalgia but by empirical and conceptual considerations sketched out in Chapters 3 and 4. Here, the reader has to take us at our word that an adequate morphological description must be word-based and not morpheme-based. After Chapter 4 it will not be a matter of faith or trust.

The content of the description that follows will reflect the MH speaker's ability to form words from other words. As that and that alone, according to us, is morphology, we use the term *word-based* in the sub-title.

As no discussion of *word-based* can be complete without a discussion of *word*, we are obliged to examine the concept here in at least a preliminary way. Several important questions are involved here.

One of these has to do with what counts as a word in a given language. There are two sides to this question: the definitional and the normative. The definitional side is concerned with domain delimitation in the sense that the issue to be resolved is (to be understood in a language-particular way) "what is a word?" Even if a universal definition of the word were possible, language-pariticular criteria for delimiting particular instantiations would have to be developed, in particular the ones dealing with the interface between morphology and syntax. A trivial example would clarify the point: languages like Eskimo and Greenlandic, and to a certain extent even Sanskrit, do not mark their word/phrase boundaries as transparently as English does. The normative question, on the other hand, is not ontological but merely confirmatory. It asks not what a word is but whether a given possible word, or sequence of phonemes, counts as a word given whatever criteria are appropriate for "acceptable word-hood" in a given language. It asks, in other words, if a given word *exists* in a given language.

The standard answer to the normative question is of particular interest here. The confirmatory procedure it invokes is "looking up the dictionary" The problem is that *the* dictionary is always only *a* dictionary. The circumstance that a candidate-word is not listed in a dictionary or in any available dictionary is normally taken to mean that the word in question does not exist. Its acceptance, in other words, is seen as a function of its prior, attested existence.

That interpretation of what might actually be an editorial failure, we believe, is misleading. The best we can do is to say that candidate X is not listed in Y dictionaries consulted. Although that response is, undoubtedly, of some use, it cannot in principle answer the question we are interested in.

The only question that can be answered is whether a given candidate qualifies as a possible word. The grounds for that possibility reside in phonology, morphology, and semantics, but not in socially constructed and implicitly normative physical objects called dictionaries.

It is important to understand this because the morphology of a speaker must not only generate the words that that speaker can be legitimately said to have or to know but also provide the possibility of his fabricating new words as and when he needs them.

1.3 *Of Social and Mental Dictionaries*

What is contained in the social object called a dictionary is a list of words no single speaker knows in its entirety. The social dictionary does not have a morphology associated with it, but a speaker's mental dictionary, generally known as the lexicon, does. The distinction is crucial.

The second major preliminary has to do with what has sometimes been called the second lexicon, the genesis of which can be traced back to Pānini's *dhātupaṭha*. Some linguists believe that mental dictionaries, or lexica, are two-part affairs: a list of words and a list of things like roots. Some proponents of the second lexicon believe in what might be called the strong *dhātupaṭha* position. It says, essentially, that all complex words are actually put together from the entries in the second lexicon. It is this "putting together" that is traditionally understood as morphology, which is standardly said to describe the internal structure of words.

We take the view that the words a speaker can be legitimately said to have or to know exist in his lexicon in their full glory and the main function of morphology is to provide rules and schemas that allow a speaker to realize his potential for creating and understanding possible words of his language. He can use these rules and schema to discover the internal structure of the words he knows but he doesn't have to as his morphological naivete amply and repeatedly demonstrates.

The connection between what we believe to be the primary role of morphology and the notion of possible word should be obvious now. The paradox that whereas morphology must be concerned with mental lexica, the linguist has access only to non-mental lexica or dictionaries must, therefore, be resolved in order to provide a morphological description.

We believe that it can be resolved by taking very common words as the basic data-base on which to base the description and by acknowledging in advance that in cases where the words in question cannot be legitimately assumed to be in the mental lexica of the speaker whose dialect is being described, the very existence of morphological rule or schema is not only precarious but also contingent. If he/she knows neither the words from which we extract the rule or schema nor other words from which the same rule or schema could be extracted, the rule or schema cannot be said to be part of his/her morphology. The risk can be minimized by considering very common words. It cannot, however, be completely avoided. The rule or schema that would relate *radius*, *focus*, *locus* to *radii*, *focii*, and *locii* in English is totally irrelevant for a speaker who does not know any of these words. The connection between morphology and lexicon, in other words, is very intimate indeed.

It is important to point out that the focus on potential and possibility is not a idealistic adventure but an empirical necessity, a necessity that allows an individual speaker to interact with other speakers and give sense to the socially defined object 'dictionary'. To see this let us consider an example, from English. If X knows the words *teach, learn, insure, direct, teacher, learner* and *director* (and not the word *insurer*), and Y knows the words *teach, learn, insure, direct, insurer, teacher, learner* (and not the word *director*), their morphologies would allow them to create and understand *insurer* and *director* respectively and hence allow all eight words to be part of their 'dictionary' (as always social).

Obviously, real-life situations are not that simple in the sense that most (social) dictionaries contain all the eight words mentioned above. But, fortunately, it is not hard to demonstrate the existence of speakers who know words that have not made their way into any dictionaries, even the specialized ones (pharmacology, nuclear physics etc.).

It is, therefore, important to understand precisely why a certain (complex) word is seen as illegal. Our point, in other words, is not to deny that typically, speakers of a language accept the verdict of the (social) dictionary and implicitly obey the sanctions enshrined in it. It is simply that these sanctions are not of the same cloth. No dictionary of English could ever list **bnik* or **nessgood* or **hospitalsize* because no speaker of English would ever make them up. The fact that *trait* is not listed in any of them as a verb is, however, anothei kettle of fish.

We are not, it must be clearly understood, claiming that there are no limits on morphological potentiality *qua* morphological potentiality. We are simply saying that socio-cultural, pragmatic, semantic constraints ought not to be treated as matters of morphology. In as much as the dictionary is a social object, it would be surprising if it could exist without a proper concern for those matters. A dictionary, in other words, is a subset of what morphology makes available. It is, we believe, unfortunate that our social practice makes us regard what morphology makes available as co-terminus with what can be said to be in the social dictionary.

The subset called the dictionary is obtained by applying, in a manner of speaking, various kinds of filters. It is of great importance to understand the nature and structure of these filters, for they, for entirely understandable reasons, clip our wings lest man's sociality crumbles. But even in willingly accepting these clips, we, as speakers, reserve the right to make dictionary makers run for their money. Quite often, we knowingly exercise that right, and with satisfaction and pleasure. Whether an individual act of this type receives the ovation of other speakers and their record-keepers, the dictionary-makers, will depend on *all* those considerations that define the relationship between language and society.

Chapter 2

THE LEGEND

2.0 *Introduction*

In as much as Sanskrit can be said to have no syntax, India's distinguished grammatical, as opposed to philosophical, tradition is concerned largely with matters of phonetics (cf. Verma 1961; Allen 1962), phonology (cf. Kiparsky and Joshi 1974) and morphology. Hindi grammarians, in other words, have had access to one of the richest traditions of morphological analysis in the world. In addition, they have been exposed to the British pedagogical, American structuralist and post-structuralist, and other traditions (Arabic and European structuralist), though these influences may, in the final analysis, not amount too much because they themselves are heavily influenced by the Pāṇinian tradition, at least in phonology and morphology. There is actually some evidence that the pedagogical focus of English missionary grammars has sometimes created only confusion.

The history of the investigation of Hindi morphology is a part of the history of the Hindi grammatical tradition. The latter has been insightfully examined by Bhatia (1987), whose thorough and ground-breaking study makes *our* task easier than it might otherwise have been.

2.1 *The Nineteenth Century*

As Bhatia rightly credits Gilchrist (1796) with the first attempt to come to terms with Hindi morphology, we shall begin our survey with him. This point *de depart* does not deny that Hindi grammars before Gilchrist may, and in fact do, have interesting and even insightful things to say about Hindi morphology. Hadley (1772), for example, can be credited with having laid the foundations for the later work on Hindi causative and compound verbs. It merely acknowledges that it was in Gilchrist that Hindi morphology first gets its place of pride.

As Bhatia (1987) points out, morphology receives only a minimal amount of attention and, that too, indirectly in the discussion of different parts of speech in the work of early Hindi grammarians e.g. Ketelaar (1698), Schultz (1744) and Beligatti (1761). The first in-depth and in many respects still impressive analysis of Hindi morphology was provided by Gilchrist (1796) in his *A Grammar of Hindoostanee Language* (Bhatia 1987:85). Gilchrist examined carefully word-formation processes in Hindi and identified the role of different suffixes and prefixes. He (1796:99) summarised, very neatly and elegantly, the changes a verbal form undergoes in different tenses – "every infinitive ends in *na* which when taken away, leaves the common contracted form of that mood or the imperative; and *this* assuming *-ta* forms the present tense and participle; which *-a* or *-ya* (when the imperative itself terminates in *-a* or *o*), the perfect tense and participle; with *ũga* the future, with *-ũ* alone the aorist, and alone or with *kərke, e, kər, ke* the preterperfect participle".To quote Bhatia (1987:85)

> On the basis of the position of affixes and changes in the base morpheme, the process of Hindi word formation is divided by Gilchrist into four categories: (1) the adjunctives, (2) the prepositives, (3) the intermediate particles, and (4) the inflective *-a*. The adjunctives and prepositives refer broadly to suffixes and prefixes, respectively. . . The intermediate particles, which connect two identical nouns. . . Finally, the inflective *-a* accounts for the productive process of deriving feminine, diminutive, and other forms, ...

Shrilal's (1855) grammar of Hindi can be seen as the Indian counterpoint to Gilchrist's European-inspired grammar. In his analysis of Hindi verbal forms, Shrilal introduces the notion of root (*dhātu*) which has two types: verbal roots (*siddha dhātu*) and onomatopoeic roots (*anukaranāmūlak dhātu*)[1]. As in the case of Gilchrist, the stem is obtained by deleting the infinitive marker *-na* forming the base for different tense forms. Shrilal views particles as nouns derived from verbs, a root thus participating not only in verbal forms but also in generating four types of nouns viz. agentive, *khelnevala* player'; objective, *mara hua* 'killed'; impersonal *marpiṭ* 'beating'; and action-denoting, *marta hua* 'beating'.

The influence of Shrilal is seen most clearly in the work of Ethrington (1871). Though using different terminology, Ethrington subscribes to Shrilal's three-fold classification of words into nouns, verbs and indeclineables (similar classification seen later in Vajpeyi 1958). Like Shrilal, he regards the infinitive and not the imperative as the basic form. His verb and tense diagram, and tense-formation table (reproduced in Bhatia 1987:115-116) are reminiscent of Shrilal's work.

The focus of all these grammarians was not the morphological processes of Hindi but linguistic realization of such conceptual categories as tense, aspect, mood and voice. It was not important whether this realization was confined to *a word* or spread across a whole phrase or a sequence of words (e.g. see Kellogg 1876/1938:106). The focus, in other words, was not on morphology; Ethrington proposed the addition of one more participle form to the four proposed by Shrilal.

Amongst the native-speaking grammarians of the same period, mention must be made of Shivprasad's (1875) grammar. Though essentially an attempt to eliminate the absurdity of having separate Urdu and Hindi grammar, it contains an interesting discussion of transitive verbs. He classifies transitive verbs into monotransitive (*ekakarmak*), double transitive (*dvikarmak*) and triple transitive (*trikarmak*). *kha* 'eat' is mono-, *bətla* 'tell' is dia- and *bətəlva* 'cause to tell' is triple transitive. He further classified transitive roots into 'inherently transitive' e.g. *kha* 'eat' and its 'derived causative root' e.g. *khɪla* 'feed' which is derived double transitive.

Shivprasad's grammar, however, pales before the much more ambitious effort by Platts (1873). He (1873:161-65) presents a very comprehensive analysis of causal verbs in Hindi. He points out that causals from intransitives will be transitive and from transitives, doubly transitive.

> Simple verbal roots are generally changed into causal bases by the addition of the increment *-a*, and into those which are doubly causal by means of the increment *-wa*, and the root is then treated as a primitive root ending in *-a*. But in some verbs the causal characteristic *-a* becomes *la*; and in others it is inserted in the root itself. (Platts 1873:161)

His discussion is reproduced below.
(To avoid any confusion, the system of transcription has been modified according to the one used in this book)

A. (i) First causal *-a*; Double causal *-va* (primitive transitive or intransitive)

Primitive Verb	*Causal*	*Double Causal*
pəɽh-na 'to read'	pəɽha-na 'to teach'	pəɽhva-na 'to get someone taught'
gɪr-na 'to fall'	gɪra-na 'to fell'	gɪrva-na 'to have thrown down'

(ii) If the root is disyllabic, the vowels of both syllables being short and that of second -ə, this -ə is dropped in the first causal.

Primitive verb	*Causal*	*Double Causal*
səməjh-na	səmjha-na	səməjhva-na
'to understand'	'to explain'	'to have explained'
pɪghəl-na	pɪghla-na	pɪghəlva-na
'to melt'	'melt' (tr.)	'to have melted'

(iii) If the root is monosyllabic but encloses a long vowel, the long vowel changes to its corresponding short vowel in both the causals e.g.

Primitive verb	*Causal*	*Double Causal*
jag-na	jəga-na	jəgva-na
'be awake'	'to wake'	'to cause to be awakened'
bhig-na	bhɪga-na	bhɪgva-na
'become wet'	'to wet'	'to have wetted'

B. If the primitive root ends in a long vowel, causal is formed by adding *-la* and double causal by adding *-lva*; the long vowel of the root is also shortened:

Primitive verb	*Causal*	*Double Causal*
pi-na	pɪla-na	pɪlva-na
'drink'	'to give a drink'	'to cause to drink'
kha-na	khɪla-na	khɪlva-na
'to eat'	'to feed'	'to have fed'

C. Intransitive roots enclosing short vowels are made transitive by changes in the enclosed vowel e.g. ə ~ a, ɪ ~ e, ʊ ~ o

Instransitive	*Transitive*
kəʈ-na	kaʈ-na
'to be cut'	'to cut'
chɪd-na	ched-na
'to be perforated'	'to perforate'
khʊl-na	khol-na
'to become open'	'to open'

He duly notes (p.163) that a few verbs form only the double causal alone e.g.

Primitive Verb	*Double Causal*
kho-na	khʊva-na
'to lose'	'to have someone lose'
ga-na	gəva-na
'to sing'	'to have somebody sing'
lena	lɪva-na
'to take'	'to bring'

He also points out (p.163) that some verbs may form the first causal by either adding *-na* or *-la* (these verbs generally end in *h, kh, th*). The second causal is always formed by *-va*.

Primitive Verb	*Double Causal*
kəh-na 'to say'	kəhla-na / kəha-na 'to cause to say'
dekh-na 'to see'	dɪkhla-na / dɪkha-na 'to cause to see'
sikh-na 'to learn'	sɪkhla-na/sɪkha-na 'to cause to learn'
sukh-na 'to get dry'	sʊkhla-na /sʊkha-na 'to cause to dry'

and that, in a few cases (p.165) transitives are formed by simply lengthening the vowel in the intransitive:

Intransitive	*Transitive*
pɪs-na	pis-na
'to get ground'	'to grind'
'pɪṭ-na	piṭ-na
'to get beaten'	'to beat'

His discussion of the tenses (pp. 138-46) is also strikingly different from that of his predecessors. He divides the tenses into simple and compound. The simple tenses are: the aorist, the past indefinite and the past conditional (or optative). 'The aorist is the only tense that is formed by means of inflectional terminations'(Platts 1873: 139) e.g. *cə l, cə le*.

These inflectional terminations are the same for both the genders.

	Sing.	Pl.
I	-ũ	-ẽ
II	-e	-o
III	-e	-ẽ

The past indefinite, according to Platts, is formed from the perfect participle, which, in the case of an intransitive verb, is inflected to agree in gender and number with its subject; but if the verb is transitive, a passive construction is employed e.g. *cəl, cəla, pi, pɪya.*

The past conditional (optative) is formed from the imperfect participle, which is inflected to agree in gender and number with the subject (p.142) e.g. *cəl, cəlta*. "Now the fact is, it is not a *present* tense at all, but a *past subjunctive*" (p.142; italics ours). There are, according to him, six compound tenses. One of these, the future, is formed by adding to the aorist, the participle *-ga*. (p.30). The formation of what he calls the remaining compound tenses falls outside of morphology. We shall, however, have occasion to refer to his treatment of the grammaticalization of time reference in Hindi later.

Platts' schemas make it clear that participles are the nucleus of Hindi verbal morphology. The *-ta* and *-a* alternation in the participles respectively mark the imperfect and perfect aspects. The tense distinctions of time are carried by the auxiliary *hæ* and *tha*. The optative is identical with the imperfect *-ta* participle and the past indefinite with the perfect *-a* participle. Aorist *-e* is the only tense marked in the verb. The future is derived from the Aorist by adding *-ga*. The future perfect involves the perfect participle in *-a* and the future of the verb *ho*. Platts' analysis suggests the following identities:

-ta: imperfect participle ≡ imperfect aspect ≡ imperfect participial adjective ≡ past conditional/optative

-a: perfect participle ≡ perfect aspect ≡ perfect participial adjective ≡ past indefinite.

Platts' (1873) discussion of nouns and adjectives is equally detailed and insightful. Gender of nouns, he notes, may be ascertained either from their *signification* or their *form*. All common nouns and proper names that denote females are feminine. He notes that whereas words ending in *-a*, *-u*, *-o*, *-pan* are generally masculine, those ending in *-i*, *-hat* or a consonant are generally feminine. In each case he also provides an exhaustive list of exceptions.

He provides a detailed discussion of the rules of gender and number changes in the nouns. He notes (p.36) that Hindi has *two* and not *eight* cases, namely, the crude form or nominative, and the oblique form, or that to which the postpositions are added.

Platts' (1873) provides a very exhaustive treatment of adjectives. He devotes separate sections to adjectival morphology of Persian and Arabic origin. This decision of his is clearly subject to various interpretations, but, given the title of his book, the most plausible one would seem to be what can be called the stratificational interpretation, insured by the use of diacritics in modern theories. He distinguishes between the *-a* ending and non *-a* ending adjectives, the former being declined like nouns.

Although empirically solid, Platts' grammar is, in some sense, an entirely expected missionary grammar of its time. For something really unusual, one has to look at Vinson (1899) whose grammar of Hindi contains an innovative section on morphology. He considers nominal morphology, a subset of verbal morphology and represents it diagrammatically as follows:

$$V=R'vm[(t\left\{\begin{matrix}p\\a\\f\end{matrix}\right\})(e\left\{\begin{matrix}p''\left\{\begin{matrix}s\\r\end{matrix}\right.\\l\end{matrix}\right.\left\{\begin{matrix}d\\i\end{matrix}\right\})]$$

$$N=R'\left\{\begin{matrix}s\\r\end{matrix}\right.\left\{\begin{matrix}d\\i\end{matrix}\right.$$

V= verb; R'= radical; v= voice; m=mood; t=tense; p=past; a=present; f= future; e=space; l=location; p" =person; s=subject; r=case; d=direct; i=indirect or oblique; N =Noun.

According to Bhatia (1987:169), Vinson views the difference between adjectives and nouns as purely syntactic. Adjectives are analyzed as the qualitative use of nouns to which suffixes are attached syntactically rather than morphologically.

2.2 *The Twentieth Century*

In this section, we shall review some of the important 20th century work on MH morphology. We shall divide our review in three parts. The first part in 2.2.1 deals with the period 1920 to 1964 and the second part in 2.2.2 with the period 1965-1995. In 2.2.3. we summarise the characteristic features of the 20th century work on Hindi Morphology.

2.2.1. *From 1920 to 1964*

The first major Hindi grammar written by a native-speaker was written by Guru (1920)[2]. Though Guru says that he is following English grammars by which he probably means missionary grammars of English, he has not allowed himself to be overwhelmed by them. He does, however, make use of insights available from these grammars. What he has really accepted without question from structuralism are the techniques of segmentation and classification, cutting available forms to smallest pieces irrespective of whether the smallest pieces so obtained can actually be said to exist in the language or not. And even this is really part of his Indian heritage.

Although Guru's (1920:123) intuitive understanding of the structure of Hindi verbs leads him to suggest that the second person singular imperative form is the basic form rather than the 'root' or 'the infinitive' when he actually examines the processes of word-formation (e.g. in Ch.4, 356-372), he posits infinitive forms as basic. Though he says that he believes that there is zero suffix invoked in the derivation of abstract nouns e.g. *luṭ* 'robbery' from the corresponding verbal forms, he derives *luṭ* from the infinitive *luṭna* through -ə suffixation. The following observations are interesting in this respect:

> *Dhātu* is defined as that basic word changes in which produce verbs. For example, in the verb *bhāgā* 'ran', suffix -ā has been attached to the basic word *bhāg* 'you run'; therefore *bhāg* is the *dhātu*, for the verbal form *bhāga*. Similarly ā 'you come' is the *dhātu* in *āye* 'came', *jā* 'you go' in *jāū̃ga*, 'I will go' and *ho* 'be' in *hoti hæ* 'happens'. When we add *-na* to the *dhātu*, we get the ordinary (infinitival) form of the verb e.g. *bhāg-na* 'to run'; *ā-na* 'to come'; *ho-na* 'to be' etc. Some people *by mistake* call these ordinary forms *dhātu*."

His predilection for neo-Pāṇinian constructs shows itself clearly in cases like the following where an -ə suffix is posited to derive agentive nouns from Sanskrit *halant* roots e.g.

Root	*Noun*	*Root*	*Noun*
cʊr (cʊrana)	cor	hər (hərna)	hər
'to steal'	'thief'	'to take away'	'every (person)'
dip (cəməkna)	dip	dɪv (cəməkna)	dev
'to shine'	'lamp'	'to shine'	'god'

True to his structural heritage, Guru (pp. 54, 330) takes the traditional distinction inflectional/derivational for granted, and suggests that inflectional affixes of case and tense are the *ultimate* affixes and nothing can be added after them. 'Derivational affixes', he claims, are not *ultimate* and 'inflectional affixes' can be added on to them. When 'inflectional affixes' are removed, he repeats the folklore, what is left is the basic word. These assumptions invite trouble which Guru simply brushes aside. For example, he discusses the expression *dinta se* 'with pity' (p.54). He says the basic word here is *din* (basic word i.e. *prakriti*, he says) and that two suffixes *-ta* and *-se* have been attached to it. *-se* comes after *-ta* but no suffix can be added after *-se*. Therefore, he says, *dinta* is the basic word. It is not clear whether the basic word is *din* or *dinta*. Notice that it is entirely possible to argue that *-se* is not a suffix but merely a postposition, but the point is that he analyses both *-ta* and *-se* as suffixes, and can offer no reasonable explanation for this ordering paradox he creates for himself.

The next natively-written major reference grammar of Hindi according to common consensus is Vajpeyi's (1958) *Hindi Shabdānushāsana*. It bears, according to Bhatia (1987:126), the stamp of its author's "independent and defiant personality which is at once the source of both his originality and shortcomings." The book is divided into three main parts, namely, *purvapithikā* (introduction), *purvārddha* (first half) and *utrāraddha* (latter half).

The introduction deals with the nature of grammar and language, the growth and development of modern Hindi and its distinguishing linguistic features e.g. word-final *-ə*, *ne* ergative, *-h* deletion and vowel nasalization. The first part deals with nouns, pronouns, adjectives, adverbs and compounding, and the latter half is devoted exclusively to a discussion of the verbal group. An appendix deals with the related languages of the Hindi commonwealth i.e. Rajasthani, Braj, Awadhi, Bhojpuri, Kannauji, Maithli and Panjabi.

Vajpeyi (1958:173) divides the words of MH into two broad categories. Nouns and verbs are words of the first order. They are free. The second order words are prefixes and indeclineables; they only serve nouns and verbs. Adjectives also follow the nouns they modify in undergoing grammatical changes. Prefixes are different from the other indeclineable words in that the latter can occur on their own in a sentence.

The guiding principles of Vajpeyi's grammar appear to be: *arthbhedāt rūpbhedāh* 'from differences of meaning arise differences of form'; he also often invokes the ill-defined and certainly egocentric principle of *karṇkaṭutā* 'what is not pleasant to hear'. The principle of repairing unpleasant sound sequences is often unwarrantedly invoked as an explanation for irregularities observed in morphology. For example, when he notices that in (1) plurality is marked both in *gəye* and *the* but in (2) it is marked only in *thi*, he says that the sequence *gəyī thī* will not be pleasant to hear:

(1) ləɽke gəye the
(2) ləɽkıyā gəyī thī

Vajpeyi's (1958) insistence that morphemes having different meanings and functions must be assigned to different categories and given an independent status leads him to posit *-ga* 'will' as a separate morpheme which, according to him, suggests certainty of action in the future. He says like the present *hæ* 'is' and the past *tha* 'was', the future *-ga* should be written separately and not graphically cliticised to the main verb as it generally is.

Basic to Vajpeyi's discussion of Hindi verbs are the concepts of *siddha* 'accomplished' and *sādhya* 'uncertain'. The *siddha* forms, according to Vajpeyi, suggest that the action has *certainly* been accomplished. The verbal forms *khata* and *hæ* are *siddha* in *ram seb khata hæ.* 'Ram eats an apple' where there is no doubt that Ram actually eats an apple. All present and past tense verbal forms having *hæ, tha* etc. are *siddha*. But there can't be anything certain about verbal forms which are imperative or conditional. These forms are therefore classified as *sādhya*. The two verbal forms show different agreement patterns. The *siddha* forms agree in number, person and gender with the subject or object noun phrase; *sādhya* forms do not, except in the future. Future is also uncertain and therefore all the forms have *-ya* irrespective of gender.

The verbal forms which show gender agreement with nouns are called *kridanta*; all the *siddha* verbs of the present and past tenses are therefore *kridanta*. The verbal forms, as in the imperatives and conditionals, which do not show such agreement i.e. the ones that are *sādhya* are called *tiganta*. Vajpeyi divides Hindi verbs into *kridanta*, *tiganta* and *kridanta-tiganta*. A large majority of Hindi verbs are *kridanta* often having a *tiganta* element as well. Notice that the burden of agreement is shared by *kridanta* and *tiganta*. Gender is marked in *kridanta*, person in *tiganta* and number in both *kridanta* and *tiganta*.

The *kridanta/siddha* and *tiganta/sādhya* distinction is made by Vajpeyi the basis of his discussion of some formal properties of verbs. *kridanta* suffixes e.g. *-ta*, *-ti* mark gender and are suggestive of accomplished activity; *tiganta* verbs are not influenced by gender distinctions.

The existential forms of the verb *hə* 'be' are analyzed as *tiganta* by Vajpeyi. He suggests that the existential root is *hə* and the third person present tense suffix is *-ɪ*, which changes to *-o* for second person and to *-u* for first person. Vajpeyi sets up *-ɪ* suffix for *tiganta* verbs suggesting imperatives, wishes, curses, blessings, possibility, etc. All past tense forms are *kridanta* i.e. gender is marked in them. Present tense forms are *kridanta-tiganta*.

The same verb can function as a *kridanta/tiganta* depending on what suffixes are attached to it and what grammatical information is coded in them.

In order to describe what are traditionally called causatives, Vajpeyi (1958:456-76) creates the category of *updhātu* (sub-roots), dividing them into two groups, *viksit* (developed) and *sankucit* (restricted). Once created, *updhātu*-s behave exactly like other verbs taking on *kridanta*, *tiganta* or both suffixes. The developed forms of the basic verbs give us causal forms whereas the restricted forms are used in sentences where the surface object is the doer of the action (*karm kartrik*). For example, in *mã bəcce ko dudh pɪlati hæ*, *pɪlana* 'to make somebody drink' is diatransitive: it takes two objects. It has two agents as well: child is the real subject; he drinks the milk, mother is the secondary subject just as the child is also the secondary object. Thus:

> Logical subject/indirect object: the child
> Surface subject: the mother
> Direct object: milk

Causal forms thus may have two subjects and two objects. But all causal forms don't have two objects; *all of them have two subjects*.

Unlike his predecessors, Vajpeyi does not regard *sɪlna* 'to stitch', *bə̃dhna* 'to get tied' as basic forms; *sɪlana* and *bãdhna* are not causatives derived from them. *sina* 'to stitch' and *bãdhna* 'to tie' are basic forms. In. *kəpɽe sɪl rəhe hæ̃* 'clothes are getting stitched', there is no subject; objects are used as surface subjects therefore *karmkārtrik* can't be the basic form. This is a *karmkārtrik* verb where the object is used as a subject.

-l insertion and 'morphophonemic changes'[3] may neutralise many distinctions:

khana	'to eat'	khɪlana	'to make X eat'
khɪlna	'to flower'	khɪlana	'to make X flower'
khelna	'to play'	khɪlana	'to make X play'

Verbal forms having the structure CV e.g. *pi* 'drink' *so* 'sleep' *si* 'stitch' *de* 'give' etc. form their first and second causals incorporating '*l*' before the regular causative suffixes *-a* and *-va*.

Vajpeyi (1958: 466) points out that a large number of verbs will not have causative forms for semantic reasons. For example, one cannot, according to Vajpeyi, make anyone lose or find something . Hence

> kho *khʊa *khʊva *khova 'lose'

Vajpeyi (1958:281) also points out that the *-ta* and *-ti* suffixes normally associated with present tense are really tense-neutral. Tense marking in predicate phrases containing these suffixes is carried by the auxiliary. Irrespective of time, these endings suggest normal, habitual state of affairs. For example

mohən skul jata hæ
mohan school goes
mohən skul jata tha
mohan school used to go
mohən səda skul jata rəhega
mohan always school will go

In the above sentences, tense is marked in the auxiliary: *hæ* (present), *tha* (past) and *ga* (future); the invariant form *jata* only indicates habitual aspect. The *-ta*/*-ti* words can also be used as adjectives as in

rota hʊa ləṛka
'crying boy'
roti hʊi ləṛki
'crying girl'

Both Guru (1920) and Vajpeyi (1958) use the structural techniques of segmentation and classification to attempt to capture processes of word-formation in Hindi. However, far more than Guru, Vajpeyi invokes subjective criteria of semantics and euphony to explain a large variety of regular and irregular phenomena in Hindi morphology. 'Different meaning, different word, different category' and 'pleasant to the ear', are the guiding principles for Vajpeyi. Guru (1920: 124) warns us against exclusive dependence on meaning and uses criteria of form and usage as well, though he creates his own confusions.

Following English school grammars, Guru discusses word-formation processes in terms of kinds and uses of words, e.g. 'inflection' and 'derivation'. He classifies words of Hindi into eight categories, four declineable *viz.* nouns, verbs, pronouns and adjectives and four indeclineable ones *viz.* adverbs, postpositions, conjunctions and interjections. In what he calls inflectional morphology (*vikār*), he deals with gender, number, case, adjectives, pronouns, verbs and compound verbs. In what he calls morphology, he deals with affixes, compounding and reduplication. Vajpeyi, on the other hand, divides the words of Hindi into two broad categories. The first order words are nouns and verbs. They are free. The second order words are prefixes and all the indeclineables serving as it were nouns and verbs.

Both Guru and Vajpeyi agree that the ultimate suffixes generally constitute a natural class that has a privileged status. They believe that this class is co-extensive with what they call *rupgāmik*. No suffix can be, they believe, added after them. However, Guru does consider expressions such as *ghər mẽse* 'from the house' as exceptions to the above rule. Vajpeyi gets around this problem by saying that *rupgāmik* suffixes can follow each other, only other 'kinds of suffixes can't be attached after 'inflectional' suffixes.

2.2.2. *From 1965 to 1995*

After the generative intervention in linguistics, it was natural for Hindi grammarians to turn to the new paradigm. Although the results of this new orientation have had a greater influence on the study of MH syntax, morphology has not gone untouched.

The desire to posit abstract underlying forms received a fresh impetus: for example, Vajpeyi's (1958:395-98) attempt to set up *hə* as the basic form for *hæ, hæ̃, hũ, tha, the* etc. is paralled by Rajgopalan (1973:60-61). In fact, the effort to collapse formal and semantic analysis often results in morphological absurdities which unnecessarily mystify the processes of word-formation.

For Guru, nouns undergo changes to mark variations in gender, number and case and verbs undergo changes to mark gender, number, voice, mood, tense and person. For the derivation of non-basic words, Guru sets up two categories of prefixes and suffixes, the suffixes being further divided into *kridanta* and *taddhita*, the former attaching to verb roots and the latter to words other than verbs. *kridanta*-s could themselves be declineable as in *ata* 'coming' (masculine) vs. *ati* 'coming' (female) or indeclineables as in *khakər* 'having eaten'.

There is no fundamental difference between the ways in which Guru and Vajpeyi describe Hindi causatives. Vajpeyi's analysis is perhaps more comprehensive in that it captures the relationship of causatives with transitive and intransitive verbs and the generalization that causatives function exactly like simple words, once formed.

He introduces the concept of *updhātu* (sub-root) which could either be *viksit* (developed) or *sankucit* (restricted), the former giving causative forms and the latter used in object-oriented constructions e.g.

Basic form: kəʈ 'cut' (kəʈna)
Subroot: kəʈ
Object-oriented (restricted) : kəʈna
First causative : kəʈana
Developed second causative : kəʈvana

The structuralist attempts to capture the word-formation processes of MH reach their apex in Upreti (1964). It is a careful and systematic account of MH affixes. According to him, two elements are required for the analysis of words, namely, *prakriti tatva* and *pratyay tatva*. Figure 2.1 (p.38) shows the further classification of these word constituents. The *prakriti* elements are the base forms. They have meaning. The *pratyay* (affixal) elements have no potential to denote either objects or emotions and can appear only in conjunction with the base forms.

The *prakriti* elements could either be 'bound' or 'free'. The bound elements consist of nominal and verbal roots, and require a *vibhakti* before they can be used in a sentence. *pad* is the inflected form having *vibhakti*.

From the point of view of affixation, basic forms may be divided into the following three categories: *mūl* 'basic', *vyutpann* 'derived' and *pad* 'inflected'. The basic forms consist of constituents which cannot be divided further from the point of view of meaning e.g. *ram*, 'Ram', *ghər* 'house' *baʈəl* 'bottle' etc. or *cəl* 'walk'and *kha* 'eat' etc. The derived forms are morphologically complex and are derived from basic or derived forms e.g. in the derived *rozgar* 'livelihood', *roz* 'daily' is basic; *berozgar* and *berozgari* could be further derived from it. The morphologically complex forms to which affixes could be attached will consist of derived verbal roots *(vyutpann dhātu)* and derived nominals (*vyutpann prātipadik*).

The derived verbal roots include denominal verbs, transitive roots and causative roots; derived nominals include nouns, pronouns, adjectives and adverbs.

The *pad* forms to which affixes could be attached include basic verbal or nominal forms or derived verbal or nominal forms.

pratyay 'affix' is defined as that part of the word which does not by itself denote any meaning and which does not have the potential to be used freely in a sentence and acquires meaning only when used with a *basic, derived* or *inflected* word. Derivational affixes are attached before or after *dhātu* or *prātipadik* to form other kinds of *dhātu*-s or *prātipadik*-s.

The grammatical affixes include terminations and enclitics. Enclitics consist of postpositions and expletives. *vibhakti* (terminations) enables *dhātu* and *prātipadik* forms to participate in sentences. For example, in

baləkõ ne	kɪtab	pəɽhi
boys	book	read

Fig. 2.1 : *Upreti's (1964) classification of word-constituents*

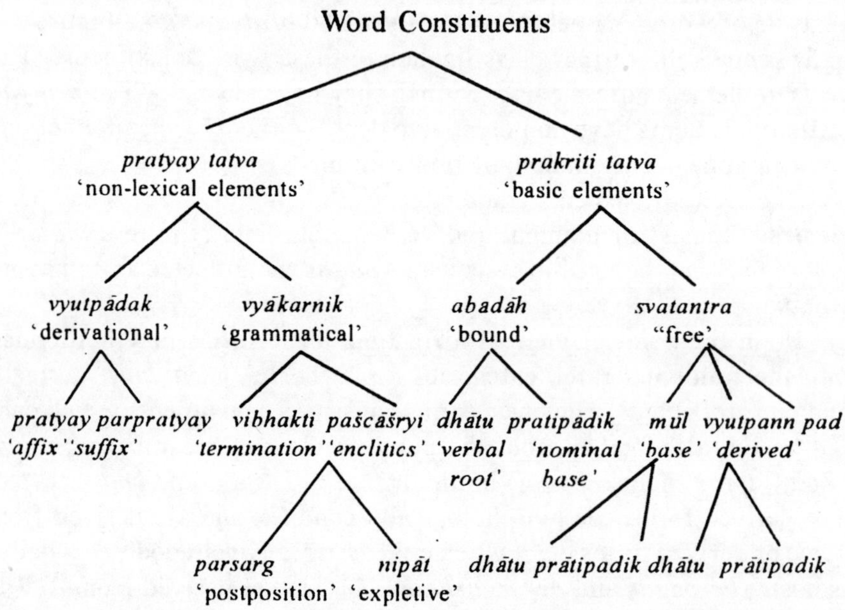

baləkõ is a nominal and *pəɽhi* a verbal *pad*. *baləkõ* is derived from the *prātipadik balək* 'boy' and *pəɽhi* from the *dhātu pəɽh* 'read' *-õ* is the termination in *baləkõ* indicating case, number and gender. *-i* is the termination in *pəɽhi* indicating third person, singular, feminine, fem past tense. Terminations are thus *pad*-forming affixes.

Enclitic affixes are those bound forms which indicate grammatical *pad*. *ne* in the above sentence, which Upreti also takes to be a word, is an enclitic as it indicates the relation between 'the boys' and 'reading'. *hi* is an enclitic in *ap hi kəhɪye* 'You EMPH say' and *bhi* is an enclitic in *calo bhi əb* 'let's go EMPH now'. Enclitics may be further divided into *postpositions* which mediate between two *pads* and *expletives* which simply modify a *pad*.

Accepting Marchand (1960), Upreti (1964:27) suggests that prefixes are adjectival in nature. In *nɪḍər* 'fearless' *kʊmata* 'bad mother', *ənmol*, 'priceless' *nɪ-*, *kʊ-* and *ən-* modify the meanings of base forms they are prefixed to; in *pəncayət* 'panchayat, local civic body consisting of five elders', *khalipən* 'emptiness', and *tirəndaz* 'archer' *-ayət*, *-pən*, and *-əndaz* are suffixes; they do not modify the meaning of the basic word. The basic word decides what the suffixes would mean e.g. *-pən* forms abstract nouns.

Following the traditional derivation/inflection distinction, Upreti (1964:29) points out that derivational affixes create new dictionary meanings while grammatical terminations elaborate grammatical relations. Inflectional affixes encode a variety of grammatical information—a termination attached to a nominal *pad* may give us information about case, gender and number; while a verbal termination may indicate voice, tense, mood, person, gender and number. Derivational affixes do not encode such information.

Derivational affixes, he believes, cannot be added after inflectional affixes (Upreti 1964:29). Affixes that follow may be enclitics, they will never be derivational. Terminations define the limits of derivational affixes. Upreti (1964:30) is forced to coin the term 'derivational inflection' (*vyutpādak vibhakti*) when he notices that the same forms may at once be interpreted as inflectional and derivational. For example, in

gəʈhɽa	kəhã	hæ
bundle	where	is

The *-a* in *gəʈhɽa* indicates case, gender and number (inflectional) but as contrasted with the *-i*, he claims, in *gəʈhɽi*, it is also suggestive of large size (derivational).

No terminations can appear between a *dhātu* or *prātipadik* and a derivational affix. Thus, **ləɽkɪyãpən* 'girls-hood' is not possible.

Terminations form *pad;* enclitics are used after *pad*. Terminations become a part of the word to which they are attached; enclitics stay independent. Terminations, in general, cannot be added after enclitics.

Though it is Vajpeyi (1958) who calls his book *Hindi Shabdanushasan*, it is Upreti (1964) who provides us a systematic, careful and detailed analysis of Hindi morphology. Upreti's work is, however, deeply rooted in the Pāṇinian and the American structuralist traditions. In Chapter 4, we have provided enough evidence to show that categories and processes such as 'base forms', 'roots', 'morphemes' and 'inflection' and 'derivation' are not relevant for morphological analysis.

Other than Upreti's (1964) landmark work and selected chapters in Platts (1873), Kellogg (1876/1938), Guru (1920) and Vajpeyi (1958), very little work was done on Hindi morphology in the structuralist framework. The amount of work produced in the generative paradigm was still less (see Singh 1994 for a survey). Kurylowicz (1960), Kelkar (1968), Srivastava (1968;1974;1987) and Ohala (1972;1983;1985;1987) among others were primarily concerned with the phonological structure of Hindi. Though D'souza (1985), Bharati (1988) and Pandey (1990) work in a non-linear model with syllable as the basic unit of analysis, their domain is essentially word-internal.

For Anjanee Singh (1994) there is an interface between phonology and morphology and problems of vowel changes and loss of vowels e.g. schwa deletion belong essentially to this interface.Working in a modified, non-linear version of the generative model, she posits a level of 'phonology', manipulated largely in terms of 'prosodic elements like the syllable, sonority, accent and well-formedness conditions'(p.254). Schwa desyllabification,for her, is triggered by affixation and explained in terms of rules of accentuation and syllable-weight. For a pair of words e.g. *ləpəṭ ~ ləpṭẽ* 'flame', one has to apply the following 'phonomorphological interface rules' on the abstract underlying forms: nasal spread, accentuation, schwa-desyllabification, resyllabification and reaccentuation (Singh 1994:209-213).Schwa-deletion is not an across the board automatic phonological process as is clear from alternate pronunciation of words like *rəjəni ~rəjni* 'night'. Ohala (1972) had to bring in a variety of diachronic and sociolinguistic considerations into play to increasingly restrict and refine the application of 'schwa-deletion rule'. For us, the process of schwa-deletion in this case is essentially morphological as it is triggered by a morphological operation on a specific set of words. It becomes an integral part of the Word Formation Strategy (WFS) that is required to explain relatedness obtaining among pairs of words in a given set. We will have more to say on phonomorphology/morphophonology in 4.5.

2.3 *Conclusion*

The brief survey above makes it clear (i) that most studies of Hindi morphology are generally embedded in fuller reference grammars, (ii) that contemporary studies deal with specific bits of Hindi morphology in order to test the validity of this or that linguistic hypothesis, (iii) that all studies of Hindi morphology are structuralist in orientation whatever the label given them by the grammarians or their critics and historians, (iv) that they all operate with typically Pāṇinian constructs such as root and stem, (v) that they do not make any systematic distinction between phonology and morphology, sometimes talking about *sandhi* as if it were phonology and at other times talking about it as if it were morphology and (vi) most of them, use a multiplicity of criteria to 'elucidate' or 'explain' morphological matters: pragmatics is mixed as easily with laws of pronunciation (cf. Vajpeyi's *karṇkaṭutā*) as synchrony with diachrony. We must, however, add that the same features can be said to characterize the morphological study of most Indic languages. It is ironic because the structuralist model of morphology par excellence has always been in the air on the sub-continent. Only Upreti (1964) comes close to being a full structuralist description. Otherwise, the quiet confidence generated by an elegant and coherent description, such as the one achieved in Kelkar (1968) for Hindi phonology, is not conveyed by anything in morphology. We offer this book as a step in that direction.

Now, we can get down to outlining the theory that guides the description that will follow. As the theory is presented and discussed in a series of articles by its architects (cf. Ford and Singh 1984; 1985; 1991), we will not attempt to fully motivate it here, partly because the motivation is provided in those articles and partly because our focus here is not the theory itself but the description that it makes possible and against which not only this but all other theories of morphology should be evaluated. We will, however, show (Chapter 4) that the theory to be utilized is fully supported by Hindi facts of the matter. The discussion of any possible, major or minor, modifications cannot be taken up here and will be addressed in the concluding chapter.

Notes

1 To avoid the stylistic infelicity of repeatedly using expressions such as "so called stem" and "so called root", we shall suspend our own disbelief throughout this chapter.

2 Guru devotes a substantial part of his grammar to the processes of word-formation. Out of a total of 584 pages, only 26 are devoted to the Hindi phonological structure and only 164 to its syntactic structure. But the processes of word-formation are dealt with in 368 pages i.e. over 63% of the volume of the book.

3 We remind the reader that this expression is to be taken exactly like "root", and "basic form" throughout this chapter i.e. with a pinch of salt.

CHAPTER 3

THE THEORY

Morphology is the study of words that are formally and semantically related. Words are, however, not given in advance: they are determined by the theory. In the theory proposed here, an expression must possess the following three properties in order to be a word[1] :

(a) a phonological structure
(b) a category
(c) a meaning

Any morphological relationship between two words of a language can be described by a rule, to be called a Morphological Strategy (MS) or a Word Formation Strategy (WFS) having the following form:

(1) $(X)_\alpha \longleftrightarrow (X')_\beta$

where

i) X and X' are words
ii) α and β are morphological categories
iii) $\longleftrightarrow$ indicates an equivalence relation (a bi-directional implication)
iv) X' is a semantic function of X
v) 'indicates a formal difference between the two elements of the relation of the morphological operation
vi) 'can be null if $\alpha \neq \beta$

The morphological relation between the two English words *cat* [kæt], *cats* [kæts], for example, is given by the following strategy.

(2) $(X)_{n,\, sing} \longleftrightarrow (Xz)_{n,\, pl}$

We call this rule a strategy because as a generalization drawn from a particular fact, it can be activated in the production or understanding of new words. A morphological strategy, in other words, captures the morphological relatedness amongst the words that happen to be in the lexicon and allows a speaker to morphologically analyze a word he may not have analyzed before or to create a new word that he may not have in his lexicon or may have forgotten temporarily. The listing of the morphological strategies of a language constitutes a part of the description of that language. It is, therefore, an aspect of linguistic competence, a component of grammar[2].

Morphological strategies alone do not account for all formal relationships. They sometimes get a hand from phonology. Each time an aspect of a formal relationship is attributable to phonology, which covers all and only global, automatic alternations governed by phonotactics, that aspect is suppressed in the morphological strategy.

In the relationship between English *cat* and *cats* as expressed by (2) above, the z~s alternation depends on a phonotactic rule of English: z→s repairs the ill-formed coda-sequence **tz* (cf. Sommerstein 1977; Singh 1987).

We can ask ourselves: why is the suppression of the z~s alternation in (2) phonological rather than morphological? One of the reasons for treating it as phonological stems from the fact that English allows *-dz* as a word-final coda, but it doesn't have any word that terminates in a *-tz* coda.

A number of constraints on the nature of morphology are implicit in the proposal outlined above:

i) *No multiple morphologies*: We reject distinctions e.g. derivational/inflectional, clitic/non-clitic, productive/non-productive, concatenative/non-concatenative, template/non-template etc. (for the latter pair, see Baker 1985).

ii) *No morphological operations on units other than the word*: Hence, no unit smaller than the word (e.g. root, stem, lexeme, basic, abstract form, etc.) can be regarded as an object of a morphological enquiry.

iii) *The unity of the morphological operation*: No segmentation of the operation to create an intermediate level of representation between morphology and phonology is allowed; hence, no morphology that implies a separation between morphology and morphophonology and no affixation-truncation (cf. Aronoff 1976), nor copying-spelling (cf. Carrier 1975) types of separation.

iv) *The operation has no privileged direction*: No special status is given to back-formation as in, for example, Marchand (1969), and Kiparsky (1982).

v) *No category is exclusively determined morphologically*: Hence, no conjugation, declension, or intra-extra-paradigmatic kind of typology (cf. Chêne 1975 or Bybee 1980).

vi) *Morphological integrity of the word*: No conditions e.g. the adjacency condition are to be entertained (cf. Siegel 1979).

These constraints may seem to be negative but we think that is in the nature of any constraint to impose restrictions and in this way strengthen the hypothesis. This should not come as a surprise to anyone. The only way to demonstrate that we do not need the excluded notions is by induction based on the analyses presented here We claim that we do not need them. The burden of proof is, clearly, on those who want to dispense with these constraints and introduce complicated devices to account for the facts.

Notes

1. Whether these properties are sufficient or not to define the word is a question that we shall leave open. They are necessary but insofar as we wish to distinguish between syntax (formal relationships between units other than the word) and morphology, they are probably not sufficient.
2. It seems necessary to state this since the type of analogical process that results from the application of a morphological strategy in the production of a new form has been characterized as being extra-grammatical (Bever, Carroll and Hurtig 1976; Carroll 1974). According to these authors, the sentences of any language always contain a number of acceptable but ungrammatical sentences. Among these some have a corresponding grammatical form and are only errors. Others seem to be perfectly acceptable.

(1) Bill will try and do it = Bill will try to do it.
He's good and willing = He's very willing.

According to them, these structures and others are resistant to syntactic analysis. They are examples of analogy (the extensions of existing forms to new functions). We reject the dichotomy.

CHAPTER 4

MORPHOLOGICAL THEORY AND MODERN HINDI

4.0 *Introduction*

In this chapter, we shall try to show that the facts of Hindi word formation are fully consistent with the various claims of the theory briefly outlined in Chapter 3. The details of this theory were worked out in Ford and Singh 1984, (1985 and 1991). Though 'Projection Model' and 'Integral Listing Model' (see Martohardjono and Singh 1992) have been proposed as two possible names for this theory, we will, taking a suggestion from Ford and Singh (1985), refer to it as the 'Word-Network Model' The new name, we hope, underlines two major aspects of the theory viz. words are the basic units of morphological analysis and related words are best described in terms of complex word-networks.

4.1 *Of Words and Word-Parts*

Most morphological theories assume the existence of units smaller than the word, be they morpheme, lexeme, root (*dhātu*), stem, base form or basic word (*mūl šabd*)[1]. The morpheme, traditionally defined as the minimum meaningful unit, has really been the basis for most of the influential morphological analyses that we know of. A by-product of structuralism, it is isolated using the techniques of segmentation and classification, all in the final analysis derived from Pāṇini. In the Word-Network Model, the "morpheme" as a minimal unit of meaning has no place. The basic units of analysis are words and word-parts (which may or may not have meaning but certainly have no lexical status outside of the word-formation strategies in which they figure as variables or constants). Though word-parts in many cases will correspond to what are traditionally called morphemes, there are, as it will soon become clear, many word-parts in WFSs that cannot be classified as morphemes. Ford and Singh have shown that different conceptions of the morpheme whether European or American do not define the same set. The European structuralists (e.g. Martinet 1960; Hjelmslev 1963) view it as a minimal structural unit which happens to have meaning. The American structuralists (e.g. Bloomfield 1933; Nida 1946; Hockett 1958) view it as a set of allomorphs and as the minimal meaningful unit of grammatical analysis. A process-oriented

(Kurylowicz 1949) definition views the 'morpheme' as the active part involved in the processes of word formation. The question of meaning is not relevant here. The fact that these conceptions of the morpheme define different sets may be illustrated from the Hindi data in (1):

(1) *Related Nouns and Adjectives in Hindi*

Noun (nom, masc, sing)			Adjective (Xless, X = Noun)	
1.	adhar	'base'	nɪradhar	'baseless'
2.	bhəy	'fear'	nɪrbhəy	'fearless'
3	-	-	nɪrbhik	'fearless'
4.	pap	'sin'	nɪšpap	'sinless'
5.	ḍər	'fear'	nɪḍər	'fearless'

According to the static European definition, *nɪr* in 1 and 2 is a morpheme which forms adjectives from nouns and has the meaning 'Xless' where X is the noun in question. But in 3, *nɪr* can't be a morpheme since *bhik* does not exist in Hindi. Thus, in spite of semantic and formal similarity, we are forced to treat the *nɪr* in 3 differently from the *nɪr* in 1 and 2. For the dynamic European definition, *nɪr* in 1, 2 and 3 is a morpheme because it participates in the processes of word formation. The *nɪš* in 4 and the *nɪ* in 5 will be treated as separate morphemes. For the American structuralist, *nɪr, nɪš* and *nɪ* must be interpreted as allomorphs of a single abstract morpheme. Different definitions, thus, define different sets. The concepts of *dhātu* (root) and *mūl šabd* (basic word) used by most Hindi grammarians (Guru 1920; Vajpeyi 1958; Rajgopalan 1973 among others) leads to similar problems. For example, Vajpeyi (1958: 395-98) sets up *hə dhātu* (root) as the basic form for not only the present tense *hæ, hæ̃* etc. but also for the past tense *tha, the* etc.

It is only the dynamic European definition which brings out clearly the formal aspects of word-formation processes. Ford and Singh's view of words and word-parts comes very close to theirs. However, given the present confusion about the concept of the morpheme, they use the term word-part only, a usage that we shall follow. Word-part is, to repeat, not a minimal meaningful unit of morphological analysis; it is simply that part which participates in word-formation processes irrespective of whether it can be said to have meaning or not.

In the Word-Network Model, word-parts are invariably associated with specific WFSs. They are introduced by morphological operations of adjunction, substitution and deletion. The Hindi data in (2) below illustrates adjunction.

(2) (X)n. abs. sing ⟷ (əX)n. abs. sing. *opposite of X*
səty əsəty
'truth' 'untruth'
səhmətı əsəhmətı
'agreement' 'disagreement'

In (3), the word-part *-ək* has been adjoined at the end to characterise another set of nouns related to each other :

(3) (X)n. masc. sing ⟷ (Xək)n. masc. sing. *doer of X*
sʊdhar sʊdharək
'reform' 'reformer'
lekh lekhək
'essay' 'writer'

We don't need to specify case in (2) and (3) since the forms of these sets of words remain invariant across nominative, oblique and vocative singular. In (4), a word-formation strategy of substitution is used involving the word-parts *-a* and *-i*:

(4) (Xa) adj. masc ⟷ (Xi) adj. fem
kala kali
'black' 'black'
moṭa moṭi
'fat' 'fat'

If in strategies (2) and (3) above, one examines the bidirectional schema from right to left rather than from left to right, one will notice processes of deletion at work. A strategy of deletion (or, from the right, of adjunction) in (5) captures the relation between a set of nouns and verbs in Hindi.

(5) (Xai) n. nom. fem. sing ⟷ (X) v. imper
ləṛai ləṛ
'fight' 'fight'
bʊnai bʊn
'knitting' 'knit'

Ford and Singh do not see any point in dividing morpheme types into classes of stems and roots (cf. Wurzel 1970; Lieber 1981), nor do they think that morphemes show preferential affinity with different classes of affixes. Rather, the shapes of 'word-parts' are constituted of the particular word-formation strategy they fall out from.

Notice that the Word-Network Model does not question the analytical capacities of the speaker. On the contrary, given the kind of schemas outlined above and the networks shown towards the end of this book, we feel that the speakers manipulate these words very creatively in understanding and forming possible though non-actual new words. Units smaller than the word are available to the speaker, though only as operational inputs and not as lexical objects. Such units consist however, merely of what falls out of particular word-formation strategies such as outlined above in (2) to (5), rather than constituting entities in their own right as is implied when they are given names such as 'stem', 'root', 'affix' etc. Thus given the WFS (3), a Hindi speaker may not only form the actual words *ɪpcarək* 'doctor', *paṭhək* 'reader', *nɪrdešək* 'director' etc. but also several non-actual (which simply means hitherto unattested) but possible words e.g. *vartalapək* 'negotiator', *prəharək* 'striker', *vɪharək* 'wanderer' etc.

4.2 *Bidirectionality*

Postulating morphological units smaller than the word e.g. root, stem, morpheme etc. inevitably leads one to a directionality constraint where the larger forms of words are to be derived from the shorter forms of roots etc. This position is difficult to maintain in the face of so-called back-formations such as English *edit* from *editor*. Despite concrete proposals to the contrary (cf. Venneman 1974; Jackendoff 1975 and Tiersma 1977), many studies in morphology (e.g. Bybee 1980; Kiparsky 1982, 1985) have proposed a directionality constraint on morphological operations. This unidirectionality constraint is generally stated in terms of deriving actual concrete forms from shorter, more abstract, so-called unmarked base forms. The Word-Network Model does not impose any directionality constraint, and proposes that all the related forms of a word are equally accessible to the speaker. As will become clear from our lexical networks, a speaker has the option to approach a given word in terms of a large number of interacting strategies. This principle assumes the shape of a bidirectional arrow in the formulation of localised word-formation strategies.

The evidence from language acquisition and diachrony would seem to support the bidirectionality hypothesis. In acquiring a language, it is not necessary to learn a simple form before a complex one. The process is certainly not linear and additive.

Learning a plural form of a noun will effortlessly give access not only to its corresponding singular but also to change in its shape due to case and gender markings as long as the relationship between the singular and the plural is formulable as a WFS. The cases of suppletion are, of course, irrelevant (cf. Singh 1992). Exposure to any one form of a verb is enough to master the whole paradigm woven around it.

Facts from diachrony also tend to support the bidirectionality hypothesis. That is, if we postulate (6) as the general form of a WFS,

(6) XA ⟷ XB

we would expect that for a stage E of a language, one would find a later stage F where new words of the XA type related to XB as well as XB type words related to XA would exist. The examples in (7) show this from the history of Hindi.

(7) Stage E

rat	'night'	ratẽ	'nights'
mala	'garland'	malaẽ	'garlands'

Stage F

kar	'car'	karẽ	'cars'
rel	'train'	relẽ	'trains'

Given the set of data from Hindi in (8), many linguists will claim that words on the right derive from the words on the left.

(8)

cəl	'walk'	cəlta	'walking'
lekh	'essay'	lekhək	'writer'
ləɽ	'fight' (v)	ləɽai	'fight' (n)
šɪkša	'education'	šɪkšək	'educator'
ləɽka	'boy'	ləɽke	'boys'

It may also be argued that both the forms in (8) derive from a third, more abstract independent form. Instead of the bidirectional representation.

X ←→ X'

the schema, one might argue, looks like the one given below

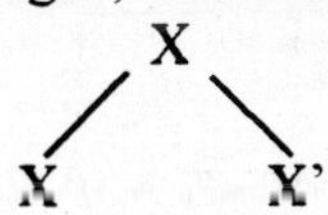

i.e. for the pair *cəl*, *cəlta* in (8) above, *cəl* is abstracted out as the root from which are derived the verb *cəl* (perhaps through zero suffixation) and the imperfect participle *cəlta* (through *-ta* suffixation).

Similar treatments have been proposed for English word formation processes. For example, for the data in (9),

(9)	evacuate (v)	evacuee (n)
	nominate (v)	nominee (n)

Aronoff (1976) proposed that the noun derives from the verb by suffixation of *-ee*. A process of truncation then deletes *-ate*. Kiparsky (1982), rejecting any truncation process in morphology, proposes another analysis according to which the pairs of words in (9) are derived separately from a unique source by two different word formation rules: a rule of *-ate* suffixing to form the verb and a rule of suffixing *-ee* to form the noun. The domain of application of these rules would be a set of abstract roots *evacu, nomin* etc. Kiparsky's position forces us to do away with strategies of truncation in general and to posit abstract forms which no speaker would recognise. These facts can be, however, straight-forwardly accounted for via substitution and, Kiparsky gives no conceptual reasons for which substitution must be ruled out as a morphological operation. His arguments against truncation may be valid but they are irrelevant for a substitution account.

The Word-Network Model completely dispenses with the notion of postulating any abstract forms in morphology and states the WFS only in terms of words and word-parts. Following Kiparsky, for the pairs *lekh, lekhək; šɪkša šɪkšək* in (8), we will be forced to posit not only roots like *lekh, paʈh, ʊpcar* etc. but also roots like *šɪkš-, prəšəns-, pərikš-* etc. We feel that the lexical relatedness of such pairs is best captured by the following two bidirectional WFSs, one involving adjunction and the other involving substitution.

(10) $(X)_{n, sing, masc} \longleftrightarrow (Xək)_{n, masc, sing}$, *doer of X*

lekh — lekhək
'essay' — 'writer'
upcar — upcarək
'treatment' — 'doctor'

(11) $(Xa)_{n, fem, sing} \longleftrightarrow (Xək)_{n, sing}$, *doer of X*

pərikša — pərikšək
'examination' — 'examiner'
šıkša — šıkšək
'education' — 'educator'

Another possible response to the data in (8) is : what is involved here are two different processes, one syntactically motivated (inflectional) as in *lərka, lərke* (no further suffixation, it is argued, is possible here) and the second lexically motivated (derivational) as in *lekh, lekhək* (where inflectional suffixes may be added to the derived form). As will become clear in 4.3, no definite criterion can be offered to distinguish between inflection and derivation. As Singh and Ford (1980) point out, this distinction only constitutes an unjustified case of interference of functionalism in the domain of formalism. Irrespective of what functions they perform in syntax, all words are formed through bidirectional WFSs.

The most frequent response to the sort of data presented in (8) is of course one of claiming unidirectionality, rooted as it is deeply in both the Western and Indian linguistic traditions. The 'word and paradigm' model claims that at least part of morphology, the inflectional part, must be represented by a set of forms in a paradigm where each form is directly related to a privileged form, called the basic word, leading word, or, more recently, lexeme. In the Pāṇinian tradition, on the other hand, what was isolated was not an actually attested word as in the 'word and paradigm' model but an abstract entity called *dhātu* (root) from which were then derived different forms of the paradigm. It is clear that in both the traditions unidirectionality of operation is accepted without any question.

The Greek, Latin and Sanskrit declensions and conjugations are indeed the classic examples of paradigms. The shortest form in the paradigm is invariably treated as the basic form in the Greek and Latin traditions. Other forms of the paradigm are derived using a set of formulas having only two types of formal operations, an identity operation later called 'zero' and an affixation operation. Other mechanisms such as multiple basic forms and replacements or suppletions were often used when these two operations could not account for all the forms in a given paradigm. As Ford, Singh and Martohardjono (in press) show, this model ran into trouble when faced with clear cases of substitution.

An ideal morphological description one so often comes across in Sanskrit grammars resembles the paradigm (the dual and plural forms are not included) in (12) :

(12)	Root :	kəm (masc) 'wishing'
	Stem :	kamə 'love'
	sing	
Nom	kaməs	(-*s* suffixation)
Acc	kaməm	(-*m* suffixation)
Inst	kamen	(-*en* suffixation and -*ə* deletion)
Dat	kamay	(-*ay* suffixation and -*ə* deletion)
Abl	kamat	(-*at* suffixation and -*ə* deletion)
Gen	kaməsyə	(-*syə* suffixation)
Loc	kame	(-*e* suffixation and -*ə* deletion)
Voc	kamə	(identity with the stem)

This well-known root and paradigm model first derives the stem or the crude base form (*prātipadik*) from the root using *guṇa* and *vṛddhi* and then adds various case and number terminations to the stem. If we add the dual and plural to the paradigm, we get a total of 24 forms related to the stem *kamə*. And yet this paradigm tells us nothing about the strategies used to obtain these forms: nor anything about the lexical relations that so transparently obtain *among* different case and number forms; nor does it capture the relations of this base with words in other grammatical categories; nor does it explain how a speaker can successfully create not only all the nominal forms but also all the related forms in other grammatical categories even if he has access to only one of these forms. Further, it is generally believed that the root by itself cannot appear as a word, being abstract in nature. Monier Williams (1857:48) points out, 'roots are not unfrequently used by themselves as substantives and adjectives, and are very commonly so used at the end of compounds'. Roots in Sanskrit really stand at the centre of a very large family of words which may include nouns, verbs and adjectives. Notice that Sanskrit case-endings may often be used to form indeclineable adverbs e.g. the locative in *prəbhate* 'in morning'; ablative in *durat* 'at a distance'; instrumental in *cıren* 'for a long time'; and the nominative in *səmipəm* 'near'. We then need multidirectional strategies to capture this network of relations (cf. Robitaille 1986 and Ford and Singh 1985). At a microscopic level, we use a bidirectional schema to capture lexical relatedness. The obvious relations among the different words in (12) can be most effectively captured, we believe by using strategies of adjunction and substitution e.g. in (13) and (14):

(13) $(X)_{n,\ masc,\ sing,\ voc} \longleftrightarrow (Xs)_{n,\ masc,\ sing,\ nom}$

Condition : X ends in ə.

kamə	kaməs
'O love !'	'love'
devə	devəs
'O God !'	'God'

(14) $(Xə)_{n,\ masc,\ sing,\ voc} \longleftrightarrow (Xen)_{n,\ masc,\ sing,\ inst}$

kamə	kamen
'love'	'for love'
devə	deven
'God'	'from God'

The relation between say the instrumental and genitive is not seen in terms of the vocative or some other basic form or root. They are seen as two independent words related through a WFS of substitution:

(15) $(Xen)_{n,\ masc,\ sing,\ inst} \longleftrightarrow (Xsyə)_{n,\ masc,\ sing,\ gen}$

Formulation of such WFSs credits the speaker with the ability of creating what for others must be actual words and what for some, perhaps even for the majority, non-actual possible words of the paradigm (and the related words not included in the paradigm) using strategies of identity, adjunction and substitution. Arranging words in a paradigm for pedagogical purposes is one matter; capturing processes of word-formation quite another.

Hindi grammarians, though influenced by western structuralism and English grammars (themselves influenced by the Greek and Latin models), often based their analysis of Hindi on Sanskrit. In spite of the fact that Hindi does not mark different case distinctions in the noun, almost all Hindi grammarians present the Hindi case termination paradigm based on the Sanskrit model (cf. 12 above). This inevitably involves including postpositions in the paradigm. With minor modifications, (16) may be considered a nominal paradigm representative of most Hindi grammarians (cf. Guru 1920:220) and Kellogg (1876/1938:106):

(16) nɔkər 'servant'

Case	*Sing*	*Pl*
Nom	nɔkər	nɔkərõ ne
Acc	nɔkər ko	nɔkərõ ko
Inst	nɔkər se	nɔkərõ se
Dat	nɔkər ko	nɔkərõ ko
Abl	nɔkər se	nɔkərõ se
Gen	nɔkər ka/ke/ki	nɔkərõ ka/ke/ki
Loc	nɔkər mẽ/pər	nɔkərõ mẽ/pər
Voc	he/əre nɔkər	he/əre nɔkəro

It should be clear from (16), the burden of case marking is carried almost exclusively by the postpositions rather than by the changes in the forms of the nouns themselves. The form *nɔkər* remains absolutely unchanged in all the cases in the singular. The *-õ* adjunction in the plural (except in the case of the vocative) marks plurality rather than case, which is marked by the postposition. As Singh (1978:73-74) has shown, in a sentence like (17),

(17) Ram ka nɔkər purana tha
Ram of servant old was

the fact that we recognise *nɔkər* as nominative, masculine, singular is not because of the form but by its concord in gender, number and *vibhakti* with the postposition *ka* 'of' and in gender and number with the adjective *purana* and the verb *tha*. Singh (1973) in fact, examines the case, number and gender forms of different shapes of nouns e.g. *-a* ending masc. e.g. *ghoɽa* 'horse', *-i* ending masc. e.g. *mali* 'gardner' *-i* ending fem. e.g. *ghoɽi* 'mare', etc. and concludes that the Hindi case, number and gender system could be simplified as

(18)

Case	*Sing*	*Pl*
Direct	ø	e,ẽ,a,ø,
Oblique	e,ø	õ
Vocative	e,ø	ø

He further (1973:83) argues that 'there is nevertheless an alternate way of looking at these forms'. The oblique forms, he says, occur predictably with postpositions only and the vocative forms are invariably accompanied with *he/əre* etc. or with a specific intonation pattern. We may then conclude that case is not a morphological category in Hindi and that the changes in the forms of nouns only mark number distinctions.

The lexical relatedness seen in (16) is then best expressed by bidirectional schemas as in (19-21) below:

(19)	$(X)_{n,\ sing,\ nom} \longleftrightarrow$	$(X)_{n,\ sing,\ obl}$
	nɔkər	nɔkər (ne, ko, se etc)
	'servant'	'servant'
	ghər	ghər (mẽ, ka, se etc.)
	'house'	'house'
(20)	$(X)_{n,\ nom,\ sing,} \longleftrightarrow$	$(X\tilde{o})_{n,\ obl,\ pl}$
	nɔkər	nɔkərõ (ne, ko, se etc.).
	'servant'	'servants'
	ghər	ghərõ
	'house'	'houses' (ne, ko, se etc.)
(21)	$(X)_{n,\ sing} \longleftrightarrow$	$(Xo)_{n,\ pl,\ voc}$
	nɔkər	(he) nɔkəro
	'servant'	'O servants!'
	ghər	(he) ghəro
	'house'	'O houses !'

4.3 *Derivation vs. Inflection*

As pointed out by Householder (1966), the notion of inflection used in the Greco-Roman tradition has not really been defined except in a circular fashion : inflected forms appear in paradigms and whatever appears in a paradigm is inflected. Derivation, on the other hand, is generally used as a catch-all term for everything that was considered to be an integral part of the word but was seen as not 'inflectional' in nature. The Pāṇinian tradition on the other hand did not make a distinction between 'inflection' and 'derivation'. Words, whether nominal or verbal, were created by adding appropriate terminations to stems derived from abstract roots. Whatever was not covered by nominal declension and verbal conjugation was taken care of by indeclineable words and processes of compounding.

As Singh and Ford (1980) point out, in spite of a very intense interaction between the Greco-Roman and Pāṇinian traditions, both western and contemporary Indian scholars have accepted the inflection/derivation distinction without serious inquiry. Not only that, most grammarians set out to look for different criteria to justify this distinction. Linguists such as Bloomfield (1933; 1939) and Nida (1946) and, more recently Matthews (1972) and Aronoff (1976) have tried to justify the inflectional-derivational opposition. As already pointed out in Chapter 1, Hindi grammarians like Guru (1920) and Vajpeyi (1958) maintained the distinction between inflection and derivation, referring to these processes as *rupantar* and *vyutpati* respectively. Though Guru, following the English pedagogical-grammar, divides words into eight parts of speech consisting of the declineable nouns, pronouns, adjectives and verbs and the indeclineable adverbs, postpositions, conjunctions and interjections and Vajpeyi, following the Pāṇinian tradition, divides them into three : nouns, verbs and indeclineables, both consistenly maintain the distinction between inflection and derivation. For both, inflectional affixes e.g. of case and tense are *caram pratyay* i.e. the ultimate affixes and nothing can be added after them.

This internal/external criterion is also used by Bloomfield, Nida and Aronoff among others. According to this hypothesis, an inflectional morpheme cannot be placed between a 'radical' and a 'derivational morpheme'. But examples violating this criterion may be found in all languages. Thus all the examples in (22):

(22) the English
menlike
the German
Kinderchen
the Hindi
bhagnevala 'one who is running'
kʊtte-bɪlli 'dogs and cat'
kəpṛevala 'one who deals in clothes'

include an 'inflectional morpheme' inside a compound constituent or 'derivational suffix'. 'Inflectional morpheme' is thus not always the closing suffix. As already noted, Vajpeyi gets around the problems examplified by (23) below and noted as exceptions by Guru:

(23) ghər mẽ se
house in from
'from the house'

where two 'inflectional morphemes' are seen in a row by suggesting that the principle is that inflectional morphemes can follow each other but a derivational morpheme cannot follow an inflectional one. Sharma (1958:114) suggests that forms e.g. *bhagnevala* be treated as *vala* participles. Even these constraints cannot account for the forms *kʊtte-bɪlli* and *kəpɽevala* where a plural form is enclosed within 'derivational morphemes'. Platts (1873:216), in fact, clearly states that Hindi nouns ending in *-a* must be inflected before the *-vala* suffix is added. Or, consider

(24) dhʊlai 'washing'

whose derivation in traditional terms of Hindi grammar must be described as forming the first causative from inflecting the base word *dho* 'to wash' and then adding the derivational *-i* to form a noun from a verb. It is thus clear that defining inflectional endings as the ultimate endings does not help us understand the alleged distinction between inflection and derivation.

Other criteria often cited are equally uncertain. For example, the so-called criterion of category change is only a functionalist transposition of the classical tradition. Forms such as *-ment*, *-ly* etc. in English and *-ən*, *-ai* etc. in Hindi are called 'derivational' because they change grammatical categories. Thus *-ment* in English forms nouns from verbs (e.g. *encroach, encroachment*), and *-ly* forms adverbs from adjectives (e.g. *slow, slowly*). In Hindi *-ən* forms nouns from verbs (e.g. *mər* 'die', *mərən* 'death') : similarly *-ai* also forms nouns from verbs (e.g. *ləɽ* 'fight', *ləɽai* 'fight') Yet, the adjective in Latin, the instrumental in Finnish or the locative in Cree, all have the function of converting nouns into adverbs, and are considered to be inflectional. As noted earlier, in Sanskrit also nominal case terminations are regularly used to form indeclineable adverbs.

Ford and Singh (1991) provide some diachronic arguments also against such a distinction. For example if inflectional morphemes constituted a class that was clearly distinct from that of the derivational morphemes, one would expect that there would be a direction in their historical evolution. That is to say, one would expect to see a clear tendency either of inflections not becoming derivational morphemes or vice versa. But inflection and derivation may proceed in both directions. For example, Beams (1872) traces the development of Gujarati genitive to the Sanskrit derivational suffix *-tan*.

4.4 *Of Paradigms*

It must be clear from the foregoing discussion that the notion of paradigm is, at best, a partial and somewhat distorted attempt to capture lexical relatedness. Word-formation processes form a network which is best captured through multi-directional strategies representing lexical redundancies that characterise our lexicons. As and when these networks are activated, they create models for understanding existing words and creating new words. The almost universally used notion of paradigm provides us only a partial picture of these networks.

A nominal or a verbal paradigm is generally given in terms of a basic form and a set of words which are regarded as functions of that basic form. Each form of the paradigmatic group is called an inflected form or inflection (Bloomfield 1933:210). There is a considerable amount of difference of opinion as to what the base form really is. The notion remains extermely vague. For Bloomfield (1933), it is a purely formal abstraction, a theme on which the forms of the paradigm are constructed. For Matthews (1965), it is a semantic abstraction, the basic form is the nucleus of meaning which underlines the set of forms of the lexeme. For both Guru (1920:123) and Vajpeyi (1958:388) root (*dhātu*) is that basic form (*mūl śabd*/*rūp*) which is materially present in all the inflected forms of the verb. What is often not appreciated is the fact that *dhātu*-s may themselves be used as words and that these are words or word-parts which help in creating listed and listable words not only in the case of verbs but across grammatical categories. For Monier Williams (1857:48-49), roots convey some simple idea, which appears under different modifications in the derivatives from it. And yet he notes that 'though the root may be compared to a rough block, or to the raw material, out of which nouns and verbs are constructed', yet roots may often be used as sustantives. Though the notion of paradigm may be pedagogically useful, as a model for capturing lexical relatedness it falls far short of what it is expected to achieve.

The Sanskrit verb, with at least ten tenses (if we exclude the Vedic subjunctive and regard two perfect forms as variations of the same tenses), six phases or grades of action, three persons and three numbers (giving at least 10 x 6 x 3 x 3 = 540 forms), indeed has a very complex verbal paradigm (Beams 1871:111, 1-6). What is generally not appreciated and hence not considered as a base for a theory of the processes of word-formation is the fact that formal features are shared across sub-components of the paradigm and that the shape of the so-called base root undergoes radical changes in different sub-groups. Williams (1857:129) notes that initial parts of different

CHAPTER 5

SOME RESIDUAL CONCEPTUAL MATTERS

5.0 *Introduction*

In this Chapter we take up some issues the resolutions of which have serious descriptive implications. Consider, for example, the issue of productivity, taken up in 5.1. If the productivity of a WFS is an integral part of it, it must figure in the description, but if it follows from other considerations, it can be left out from an ideal morphological description. Similarly, it is necessary to decide if a morphological description must use quasi-etymological diacritics such as ± Native (cf. 5.4 below).

5.1 *On Productivity*

It is customary in morphology to talk about the productivity of rules of. word-formation. Discussions of English morphology, for example, generally contain statements of the following sort:

1. *-z* is the most productive plural marker.
2. whereas '*-ness* attachment' is productive, '*-hood* attachment' is not.
3. the adverbializing *-ly* is a productive suffix.
4. *-ity* is not productive except when it is preceded by *-able*.

There is no question that in any morphological system some rules of word-formation can be said to apply very generally whereas others seem to apply only in a rather restricted fashion. The problem is where to ground this sort of information or knowledge. There are two logical possibilities: (1) each rule of word-formation carries, in some fashion, an index of some sort of how unrestricted it is in its applicability when the speaker who has it, applies it and (2) rules of word-formation carry no such index in the grammatical system and 'productivity effects' follow from other considerations.

The Word Network Model takes the latter position and works with the hypothesis that *ceteris paribus* all rules of word-formation are equally exploitable and are indeed so exploited, as both diachrony and synchrony amply attest. The differences in productivity effects, according to this model, follow from unmotivated collapsing of word-formation processes, rampant in contemporary morphological theorizing, distributional considerations of a particular sort, processing considerations, and other factors.

'steal', *corəyamı* 'I steal'). We thus notice that the notion of paradigm is not only vague and imprecise but it also prevents us from formulating generalizations across the lexicon. To the extent it operates with abstractions like roots, which no one uses, and presents forms in terms of neatly organised paradigms, which nobody is likely to have, it unnecessarily mystifies the investigation of the process of language acquisition.

Following the Sanskrit model, most Hindi grammarians laid out Hindi verbal paradigms in terms of tense, mood, person, gender and number. For example, see Guru (1920:286-292 for *cəlna* 'to walk') and Kellogg (1876:242-244 for *gırna* 'to fall'). Notice that it was felt necessary to tabulate the paradigm for all the tenses even though, morphologically, Hindi marks only the future and the contingent future in the main verb. The burden of tense marking is carried essentially by the auxiliary. This is parallel to creating the nominal paradigm with all the cases. Once again, the only case Hindi may be said to mark morphologically is the vocative. The burden of case-marking is largely carried by the postposition. As Vajpeyi (1958) points out, the only feature that is consistently marked in the main verb is the gender. Since person is not always marked in the main verb, Hindi grammarians are forced to use the pronouns themselves in their paradigms.

For a word like *cəl* 'walk', Guru lists 182 different verbal forms (compare with the corresponding 180 main verbal forms in Sanskrit). The formal variants of *cəl* we actually use are: *cəlna, cəlne, cəlta, cəla, cəlti, cəlte, cəlũ, cəle, cəlẽ, cəliye, cəlti, cəli, cəlnevala, cəlkar* and (if we do not wish to regard *-ga, -ge, -gi* as future auxiliaries) *cəlũga, cəlũgi, cəlega, cəlegi, cəloge, cəlẽge, cəlẽgi, cəlogi*. There are thus only 24 verbal forms involved. Among the 72 verbal forms on pages 288-89 of Guru (1920), only the following 4 words appear : *cəlta, cəlti, cəlte, cəlti*, the remaining distinctions are carried either by the person or the auxiliary. Even this number of 24 shrinks further when we realise that most of the Hindi verbal forms really involve participles viz. infinitival participles (*cəlna, cəlne*), imperfect participles (*cəlta*) and perfect participles (*cəla*). Notice that in spite of 182 entries in the paradigm, lexical relatedness obtaining between say *cəl* and *calək* 'driver' or between *cəl* and *cələn* 'behaviour' is not captured!

As already indicated above, the paradigmatic model does not constitute a natural model for language acquisition (Ford and Singh 1991) It has never been demonstrated that children actually construct paradigms during language acquisition. What seems more likely is that children formulate WFSs on the basis of data available to them and use them to understand

and create new words. Another justification for the paradigmatic model is drawn from the principles of markedness. It is argued that the unmarked forms are more basic and are acquired first. A partial list of some of the oft cited generalizations based on markedness is given in (27) below:

(27)	*Unmarked*	*Marked*
	present	preterit
	3rd person	other persons
	singular	plural
	finite forms	participal forms
	direct case	oblique case
	masculine	feminine

It is important to point out that the acquisition of the singular before the plural or of the oblique case before the direct case simply constitutes a tendency.[2]

4.5 *Morphophonology*[3]

Ford and Singh (1983) and Singh (1987) have clearly demonstrated the inadequacy of several popular positions held about the status of morphophonology in linguistic description. The Pāṇinian way of accounting for all sound alternations in terms of rules of Sandhi and the processes of *guṇa* and *vṛddhi* was revived most emphatically in *The Sound Pattern of English* (Chomsky and Halle 1968) and morphophonology came to be regarded as an integral part of phonology.

Such an approach, it was argued, would be less redundant. The phonological bias is retained even in more recent approaches e.g. *Lexical Phonology* (Mohanan 1986; Kiparsky 1982 and 1985 among others) in which phonological and morphological rules apply alternately on each other's output or, as Kiparsky (1982) puts it, 'in tandem'. The opposite classical comparativist position, that morphophonology is an integral part of morphology is seen by Paṇinians as leading to 'unwarranted redundancy'. As phonological processes are automatic, i.e. apply across the board and appeal to universal laws that repair violations of well-formedness conditions in a given language, morphophonological changes cannot be a part of phonology. They are non-automatic and are an essential part of the specific morphological operation with which they are associated. Singh (1987:280) shows how what is regarded as the regularity of velar softening in English can be captured rather straight-forwardly by a rule of word-formation that coexists with a general rule that imposes no morphophonemic modification viz:

(Xk) ⟷ (Xsity) (electric, electricity)
(X) ⟷ (Xity) (lax, laxity)

In 'Morphophonology of Hindi, 'Elizarenkova (1988) proposes to set up a separate level of morphophonology as a bridge between the levels of phonology and morphology (p.367). She, for example, proposes the following 'universal morphophonological rule' (p.269) for the Hindi nominal stems ending in *-i*:

-i + V> = ɪy V

to account for the following sets of words:

ləɽki	'girl'	ləɽkɪyã	'girls' (direct pl)
ləɽki	'girl'	ləɽkɪyõ	'girls' (obl. pl)
bhai	'brother'	bhaɪyõ	'brothers' (obl. pl)
bhai	'brother'	bhaɪyo	'O brothers' (voc. pl)

Elizarenkova's own subsequent analysis, however, shows that the 'universality' of these alternations resides in being tied to these sets of words. From the phonological point of view, there are many words in Hindi which allow the sequences of long and short vowels in any combination without any glide insertion. Words like *lai* 'brought', *roai* 'weeping', *kai* 'moss' etc. are common enough to cast serious doubts on the phonologization of morphophonology proposed by Elizarenkova (1988). The essentially morphological character of these sound alternations is underlined by the fact that both *ləɽki* and *bhai* show glide insertion and vowel shortening, but in the former case it is associated with the direct and oblique cases while in the latter with the oblique and vocative. What is involved here is a word-formation strategy of substitution albeit with some change that only appears to be phonological viz.

(Xi)n. fem. sing ⟷ (Xɪyã) n. nom. fem. pl

This strategy captures the raltionship that obtains between the pairs of words e.g. *ləɽki* 'girl', *ləɽkɪyã* 'girls'; *ghəɽi* 'watch', *ghəɽɪyã*; 'watches'; *nədi* 'river', *nədɪyã* 'rivers' etc. Similar word-formation strategies would capture the relationship between other pairs of words above. In her analysis of 'verbal word-formation' (371-377), Elizarenkova tries hard to achieve a semblance of overall regularity in the formation of causatives in Hindi using processes such as 'quantitative alternation' and 'vowel alternations'. It is not only that different combinations of these processes are associated with different sets of words but also in each case there is a large number of exceptions, enough to motivate an additional strategy of word-formation. After suggesting that vowel gradation is an essential part of forming causatives in Hindi, she goes on to point out that words having the diphthongs *-ai-* and *-au-* do not undergo any vowel gradation in forming causatives. Similarly, in the case of diminutives of nouns, some involve vowel gradation, some vowel gradation with quantitative alternation, and some do not involve any morphophonemic change e.g.

ghoṛi	ghuṛɪya	'mare'
am	əmɪya	'mangoe'
bora	borɪya	'sack'

There are thus multiple ways of achieving the same morphological change and each one of these ways may or may not have sound alternations associated with it. Any attempt to present these strategies in the garb of "phonological rules" will only lead to statements involving expressions such as 'generally', 'most of the times', 'except in the following words', 'but.' These formations are morphological formations par excellence.

Notes

1. In this chapter also we shall suspend our disbelief and use words such as root, morpheme, stem, inflection, and derivation for reasons of comprehensibility and stylistic felicity.

2. One may say that our critique of the paradigm, taken over from Ford and Singh (1991), may be valid only for inappropriately set up paradigms. If paradigms are set up appropriately, i.e. motivated by Hindi and not by Sanskrit or Latin, They can, it may be claimed, be revealing indeed. Paradigms based on languages or grammars other than the one being described cannot, of course, be taken seriously. Even internally-motivated ones, we are pleading, provide only a partial picture of lexical relatedness, a picture from which some crucial matters of that relatedness are, unfortunately, invariably, left out, though some of these matters can, we admit, be directly inferred from the paradigm-based picture. As we do not have sufficient space here, we invite the reader to look at Ford and Singh (1991) for some examples, from Latin, of lexical relatedness generalizations the paradigm seems unable to capture.

3. The term *morphophonology* is used here and throughout the rest of this book as a word borrowed from discourses other than that of the theory espoused here. It should also be taken with a pinch of salt, as should its relatives (*morphophonemic*, *morphophonology* etc.) We shall, however, continue to use it and its relatives without any quotation marks or awkward honorofics like *so called* for pedagoical reasons.

CHAPTER 5

SOME RESIDUAL CONCEPTUAL MATTERS

5.0 *Introduction*

In this Chapter we take up some issues the resolutions of which have serious descriptive implications. Consider, for example, the issue of productivity, taken up in 5.1. If the productivity of a WFS is an integral part of it, it must figure in the description, but if it follows from other considerations, it can be left out from an ideal morphological description. Similarly, it is necessary to decide if a morphological description must use quasi-etymological diacritics such as ± Native (cf. 5.4 below).

5.1 *On Productivity*

It is customary in morphology to talk about the productivity of rules of. word-formation. Discussions of English morphology, for example, generally contain statements of the following sort:

1. *-z* is the most productive plural marker.
2. whereas '*-ness* attachment' is productive, '*-hood* attachment' is not.
3. the adverbializing *-ly* is a productive suffix.
4. *-ity* is not productive except when it is preceded by *-able*.

There is no question that in any morphological system some rules of word-formation can be said to apply very generally whereas others seem to apply only in a rather restricted fashion. The problem is where to ground this sort of information or knowledge. There are two logical possibilities: (1) each rule of word-formation carries, in some fashion, an index of some sort of how unrestricted it is in its applicability when the speaker who has it, applies it and (2) rules of word-formation carry no such index in the grammatical system and 'productivity effects' follow from other considerations.

The Word Network Model takes the latter position and works with the hypothesis that *ceteris paribus* all rules of word-formation are equally exploitable and are indeed so exploited, as both diachrony and synchrony amply attest. The differences in productivity effects, according to this model, follow from unmotivated collapsing of word-formation processes, rampant in contemporary morphological theorizing, distributional considerations of a particular sort, processing considerations, and other factors.

Let us consider the *-z* plural marker in English. It is true that it not only appears in a rather large number of plural nouns most speakers of English are likely to have in their mental lexica but also more likely to show up in neologisms or non-sense words. This 'productive' behaviour, however, follows straightforwardly from the fact that the nouns whose plurals end in *-z* have nothing in common. Some of the other 'plural markers' in English, ablaut and identity, for example, have serious form-related or pragmatico-semantic restrictions. The former is restricted to rhymes of a particular sort (*foot, goose* etc.) and the latter to 'huntable' animals and some inanimate nouns of a particular sort (*sugar, milk* etc). The *-z* plural is generalized, or productively used, not because the relevant rule is marked as productive in the morphology of English but because, unlike other rules of pluralization, there is no cohesiveness of form or sense in the nouns the plurals of which do terminate in *-z* in the mental lexica of most speakers of English.

The full import of the 'default' nature of the *-z* plural in English can be better appreciated in the light of additional facts of the following sort: (1) in German, which has half-a-dozen rules of pluralization not as severely restricted as English rules of identity, ablaut, and '*-en* attachment', plural is marked with *-en* and umlaut quite as often as it is marked with *-s* and (2) given the right structural configuration, speakers of English can and in fact do use an 'unproductive' rule they are not *supposed* to – the plurals of *mongoose*, quite predictably, are: *mongeese* and *mongooses.* The latter also because there is no reason to exclude *mongoose* from the "class" *cat, house, paper, brother,* and *book* – there is in fact no class – and some reason to include it in the class of *foot* and *goose*.

There is again nothing mysterious about the fact that *-ity* is somewhat less productive than *-ness*. That result follows straightforwardly from the fact that whereas the former is often associated with a 'morphophonological' change, the latter leaves that which it 'attaches' to in its pristine transparency. This not withstanding, English speakers are known to have come up with /musikizm/as well as /muzisizm/ when attempting to coin an *-ism* word from *music*. The former results from 'plugging' the word into [X] ⟷ [Xizm] and the latter by plugging it into [Xik] ⟷ [Xisizm]. It, obviously, fits into both the general and the particular strategy.

Word-formation processes are sensitive to very subtle distinctions and restrictions and the talk about productivity is often based on ignoring them. Consider, for example, the deadjectivization process in English that forms verbs in English and has its reflex in *-en.* One *could* say that it is not a very productive process but only if one ignores the fact that the process is restricted to adjectives that terminate in consonants (hence **yellowen*, **bluen* etc.). It might actually be sensitive not only to the presence of a consonant but also to consonants of a particular type (cf. **palen*, **beigen* but *whiten* and *redden* etc.).

Considerations like moraic weight, accentuation, and pragmatico-semantic interpretative constraints are part of the *ceteris paribus* that play a role in making a word-formation process *appear* to be 'productive' or 'non-productive'. If these considerations are ignored in the formulation of these processes, they would obviously be *expected* to be more productive than they actually are, and hence labelled 'unproductive'. A word-formation process must be formulated *only as generally as is warranted* by the lexicon for which it is being formulated. The part about the licensing by the lexicon is often forgotten and the process is formulated in a very general way, later leading to the 'discovery' of its 'unproductiveness'.

The lexical license requirement is most flagrantly violated by the desire to set up Aristotlean objects with their essences neatly tagged with them. Consider, for example, what is generally referred to as 'English *-ity*'. It is quite clear that the morphological operations part of which find their imprints in the appearances of *-ity* involved in *electric, electricity* and *mendacious, mendacity* are quite different, both in form and in semantic interpretations associated with them. Yet the Aristotlean quest leads one to speak of 'the English *-ity*'. This quest ignores the fact that formal reflexes of morphological operations have no existence or meaning outside the set of words in which they find their homes.

Then, there is the question of social and normative filters. A word produced according to some sensitively and adequately formulated word-formation process may still strike some as awkward or impossible. Such judgements, however reflect only norms or fashions and cannot be used to measure the 'productivity' of that rule. The appeal to the dictionary is a redundant excercise because if one has to look a word up to find out if it is possible, one need not bother because the question has already been answered in the affirmative. Judgements of 'awkwardness' are even more patently normative judgements, if not indices of the linguist's deafness.

Productivity is, to conclude, a matter of general processing and social considerations and merits no place in morphological competence. To say this is not to say that morphological performance needn't be talked about. It is simply to say that it needn't be talked about in grammar (morphology, in this case). We shall, accordingly, have nothing to say about it in the description that follows.

5.2 *Neo-Pāṇinianism Revisited*

As it is possible to raise several other neo-Pāṇinian questions regarding the theory which has been motivated above and guides the description that follows, sometimes disguised as questions of what some refer to as 'computational linguistics', it is incumbent upon us to anticipate them and to answer them. The first of these has to do with what neo-Pāṇinians and their contemporary "computational" cohorts refer to as the derivational 'base'. Given a set of related forms like English *kill, kills, killed, killer,* our contention has been that they are related somewhat as follows:

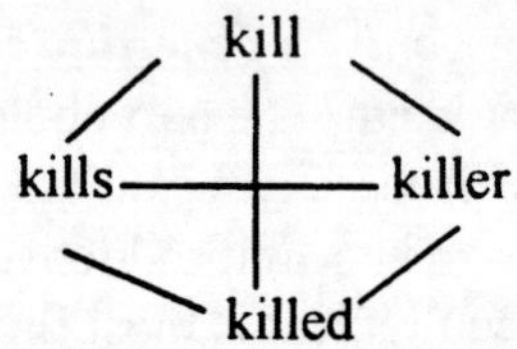

The apparently 'neutral' shape of *kill* has no privileged status in the mini-net-work of relationships above. The neo-Pāṇinians and their contemporary *avatars* will, however, like the relationships involved to be mediated via the allegedly neutral shape *kill*, perhaps, somewhat as below:

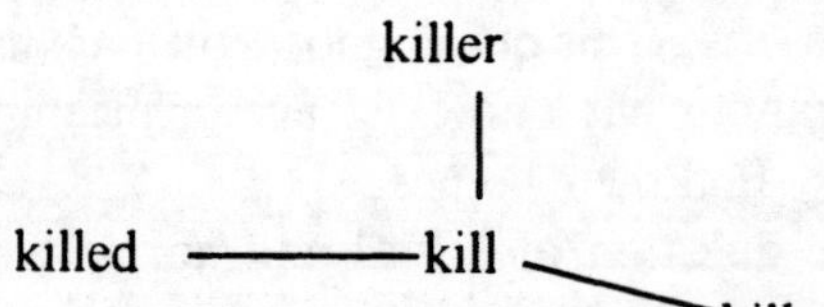

Even when they grant bidirectionality, they want to maintain the supremacy of the 'base form' as, they claim, it embodies 'economy of computation (derivation).' That claim requires that all related forms be mediated via the base. The relationship between, say, *killer* and *kills* is, according to them, mediated through 'the base' *kill:*

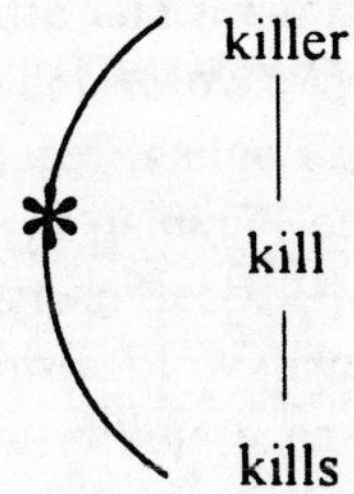

Notice that the relationships mediated through *kill* above create the illusion that it is in fact the word that is the point of departure, but it is only an illusion, because the neo-Pāṇinians *cannot* subscribe to the *pada* or word as the basic unit faced with a language even modestly richer in its morphology than English. In any language in which the nominative is identical with the vocative or the accusative with the dative, they will be forced to postulate a stripped 'base', called *aṅga* in the Pāṇinian tradition and forego expressing direct relationships of the sort these identities embody. Schematically, the relationship between, for example, the nominative and the vocative will have to work as follows:

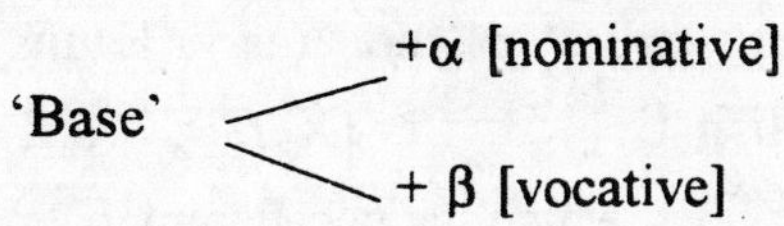

The illusion that it is possible to operate with words in the English examples *kill, kills, killed, killer* is an artefact resulting from the fact that the *aṅga* (stem) *kill* in English also happens to be a word in this language which is morphologically remarkably poor. Any so-called 'richly inflected' language like Latin or Sanskrit makes it clear that a truly word-based morphology cannot seriously entertain units other than the word or that the postulation of units smaller than the word, for whatever purpose, is incompatible with the view of morphology taken here.

It is, of course, possible to suggest that the 'base form' and other intermediate units are 'computational bridge-heads' set up for economy and computational ease. This begging of the ontological status of these units in the name of economy and 'computational ease' is a rather odd mixture of pragmatics and functionalism with cognitive pretensions. The possible argument that while units like the word are accessible to human consciousness the other units *are* there (though they are not accessible) also begs the ontological question. Even empirically, this curious appeal to 'conscious accessibility' runs into serious difficulties for it is not clear why the putative bases of words like *editor* and *peddler*, to take two classic examples of 'back-formation' in English, reach this level of accessibility only when they do. The early neo-Pāṇinian move, made by Halle (1973), was to say that they are marked [-lexical insertion] – a truly bizzare move by a theory allegedly concerned with word-formation. It is easy to see that the curious appeal to conscious accessibility at issue has the facts of the matter completely up-side-down. It is not that only word-level entities are accessible to human consciousness but rather only such entities can be said to exist in the lexicon. English *edit* doesn't wake up one day and surface on English consciousness — it comes into being one day through what neo-Pāṇinian dismissively refer to as the 'marked phenomenon of back-formation.' What is really marked is their theory because it cannot account for it.

It is possible for neo-Pāṇinian and their 'computational cohorts' to argue that whereas we do not *directly* admit the existence of units like the root, the stem, and the affix, we indirectly do so because our constants and variables are really like these units. A moment's reflection, however, will show that they are not, and this for several reasons. The most important of these is that our variable X can range over 'root' (as in English $[Xate]_v \longleftrightarrow [Xee]_n$), 'stem' (English $[X]_v \longleftrightarrow [Xer]_n$), word (English $[X]_{adj} \longleftrightarrow [Xai]_n$), and 'things' for which the neo-Pāṇinian tradition has no names; and our specified constants cover not only the affixes of the tradition in question but also intractable 'things' like umlaut and ablaut when they mark morphological categories, 'declensional' (nouns that end in *-a* in Sanskrit, for example) and 'conjugational' (verbs that end in *-ir* in French, for example) markers. One could, of course, supplement the neo-Pāṇinian list and add thematic markers, augumentatives, and allomorphy rules, but the point is that such entities don't seem to be required and certainly can't be said to exist.

Consider, for example, the notion of 'root'. Abstract objects like Sanskrit *kr* and English *nomin* have the peculiar property that they don't carry any category specification. Objects without category specification seem difficult to understand cognitively because cognition without categorisation is a bit of a puzzle. Or, concepts like 'stem'. To define it as word *sans* inflection begs the question, particularly given the impossibility of making the distinction derivation/inflection on morphological grounds.

The only option left for the neo-Pāṇinians is to say that these things are theoretical 'bridge-heads' through which computation is mediated. The question is: whose computation? Speakers don't seem to provide any evidence for entertaining or listing any thing other than words. The computationally oriented linguist's store-house of these bridges, sometimes referred to as the second-lexicon, may well be useful to manipulate a database for some specific practical purpose, usually in the interests of 'modernity', but what it could possibly have to do with the complex network of word-to-word relationships we have ample evidence for is hard, if not impossible, to see.

Moreover, the universe of neo-Pāṇinian computationality is a universe· of Aristotlean objects with their essences neatly tagged with them. Our claim, on the other hand, is that there are no objects like English *-ity*, French *-age*, German *-lich*, Hindi *-giri* with specific isolatable meanings, let alone warehouses where they are stored with their 'meanings' attached to them. 'The *-ity*' in English *mendacity* doesn't mean anything like 'the *-ity*' in English *electricity* and *-giri* in *sɔdagiri* and *babugiri* in Hindi cast serious doubts on there being a *-giri* anywhere other than in the words in which one can isolate the form, but then it is inseparably associated with a particular rule of interpretation. Aronoff's major insight was to hand-over the very coming into being of these 'things' to the rules that introduced them. It is no accident that neo-Pāṇinians felt compelled to 'objectify' them by giving them the same status as to words that can appear on their own. The complex processes whose reflexes these specifiable constants represent are, thus, reduced to a list of 'lexical objects', which obey the combinatorics the neo-Pāṇinian tradition calls morphology.

The need to reduce processes to an elementary combinatorics combined with a naive obsession with 'economy'— apparently the economy of those who pay for 'practically' usable goods— forces the postulation not only of ontologically dubious bases, stems, and roots but also of category-less objects and super-categories that can force the vocative to go through the nominative in order to get to its dative counterpart or the neuter to go through the masculine in order to reach the feminine. This sense of economy, we are told, avoids 'computational explosion', the pragmatist's name for his fear of human creativity.

Notice that it is not an accident that this sort of enthusiasm characterizes the work of those who talk about things like the English or the Hindi lexicon. As we pointed out in the introduction, only speakers can have lexicons. But those who pay for the computational enterprise want languages to have them. What the computational linguist does follows trivially from these imperatives. The point is not to stop her from doing it, but to insist that she can't operate under false pretense. What she can or cannot do is a legitimate index of contemporary computational machinery, but of no relevance to the morphological competence of speakers of natural languages.

Some neo-Pāṇinians argue that even if morphology is (acquisitionally speaking) initially word-based, once it is acquired it is restructured in terms of roots, bases, stems and affixes. In the final grammar, in other words, the second lexicon becomes more important than the rudimentary lexicon of words with which the child may well begin. The crucial evidence of *delisting* for this hypothesis is, however, never offered. Even if the English-speaking child begins by listing in her lexicon *cat* and *cats*, for example, she ends up with *cat* and the suffix *-z* (the latter in the second lexicon). Given the fact that there is no evidence suggesting that look-up procedures take up more or less time than computational procedures, the ones that will put *cat* and *-z* together, it is hard to motivate the implied delisting of *cats*. Delisting seems to take place only in highly irregular or quasi-suppletive n-tuples like *foot* and *feet* where the child does delist **foots*. And even in cases like this what is crucial is not the quasi-suppletive nature but the negative evidence presented to the child. Be that as it may, the point here is that there is no evidence for the sort of restructuring neo-Pāṇinians assume or assert and their computational cohorts are eager to espouse in order to underwrite their obsession with naive economy.

The real problem, it is easy to see, has to do with the appropriate construal of the ideal speaker-hearer. Because 'computational linguists' are interested in manipulating complex but finite data-bases, in the service of their pay-masters, they assume that a picture of the ideal-speaker-hearer can be constructed by attributing to him/her a large first lexicon of 'underived' lexical items, an equally large second lexicon of 'formatives', and, of course, the combinatorics they call morphology. Real speakers, however, seem to operate with words they happen to know and the generalizations we have been calling word-formation strategies they can extract from those words. Because speakers from similar backgrounds share their lexica, they end up with similar morphologies that allow them to negotiate their unshared lexica. 'High frequency' items cut across these backgrounds and endow most speakers with partially similar morphologies. The *crux* of morphology, however, is immense variation, and those who speak of the lexicon of English or Hindi have no way of accounting for that variation. Ours is a picture of real speakers; their's is a picture of some data-base. The interest the latter could have for a mentalist linguistics escapes us. It can, of course, serve this or that practical purpose, and practical purposes are important in life, but instrumentalization of knowledge is different from knowledge itself. These two conceptualizations should never be mistaken for each other. The description that follows is, accordingly, intended to reflect the morphological competence of MH speakers.

5.3 *On Semantic and Formal Conditions*

Our definition of a word-formation strategy as (an exploitable) generalization based on a mini-lexicon (the set of words a speaker can be said to have) requires that WFSs be formulated only as generally as the relevant mini-lexicon would permit. The generality of a WFS is subject to formal (form-related) and interpretive constraints. The rule of comparative '*-er* attachment' in English, for example, is restricted by moraic weight, and 'declensional' and 'conjugational' restrictions that abound in traditional morphological descriptions of Indo-European languages are purely form-related restrictions on 'the base'. The *-o* plural in French, to take another example, is relevant only for nouns that end in *-al*.

It is possible to say that certain WFSs are semantically restricted, as we ourselves say later in the description that follows about, for example, the non-honorific kinship terms terminating in *-a*. There is, however, an interesting class of WFSs in which the apparent semantic restrictions are not tied down to any formal property of the words involved. Consider, for example, the case of identity plural in English. In the case of count nouns, it may be said to be restricted to huntable/edible animals (deer, for example). The question that such purely semantic restrictions pose is whether they need to be stated as conditions on the WFSs involved. The fact that the $[\text{deer}]_{sing} \longleftrightarrow [\text{deer}]_{pl}$ identity is not generalized to *dog* can be expressed in two ways: (1) we can state the restriction on the relevant rule of identity or (2) not state that condition on the WFS in question but rule out the putative $[\textit{dog}]_{pl}$ on the basis of the semantico-pragmatic filter that can be assumed to exist in the Anglo-Saxon culture, which does not include *dog* as a member of the class which includes *deer*.

There is much to be said in favour of the second alternative. First, it builds in a certain potential for metaphoricity within the word-formation process, allowing the results to be filtered through interpretive and pragmatic considerations. The question in many ways is similar to the question of the status of what used to be called 'selectional restrictions' in generative syntactic theory. These have been argued out on the grounds that interpretability is a necessary condition on logical form.

In morphological descriptions, however, the convention is still to incorporate such considerations into word-formation processes. We accept this convention in the description that follows, partly because we have not written rigorous rules of interpretation for the strategies that figure in that description and partly because a principled decision to the contrary requires an extensive theoretical discussion of what might be called the limits of metaphoricity. We must, however, point out that it will not escape the careful readers' attention that considerable 'play' is possible with semantic restrictions and virtually none with form-related restrictions.

5.4 *After Etmyology: On Etymological Diacritics*

The Word Network Model, which guides the description that follows, does not use familiar lexical diacritics like [± Native]. Given the fact that such diacritics are quite popular in contemporary morphological descriptions, we need to explain and justify our refusal to use them, particularly in the context of a language like Modern Hindi, which, like other Indo-Aryan languages, is often described in terms of the familiar *tatsama/tadbhava* distinction, a descriptive distinction inherited from diachronic studies, not unlike the familiar Romance distinction between *mots savants* and *mots ordinairs*.

In languages like English, the use of such diacritics is justified on the basis of the general behaviour of its relatively rich Romance lexical inheritance. It is noted, for example, that whereas *-hood* appears with words that are generally of Anglo-Saxon origin, *-ity* appears generally with words that are of Romance origin.

The trick is in the word *generally* above. What is often meant by it is "in the speech of educated, perhaps self conscious, elites, most often linguists". Such speakers, of course, have a rudimentary knowledge and awareness of such etymological matters. Amongst the ordinary speakers, one does, however, find forms like *ill-formity*, something that can and has been used by an elite speaker for special effect (Fillmore: personal communication).

The attestation of "cross-over" cases like *ill-formity* is complemented by the existence of such honest-to-goodness words as *priesthood* (*priest* is unquestionably of Romance origin). What the advocates of lexical diacritics say in cases like this is that the 'stem' has been nativized. *Priest*, in other words, has been Anglicized. What this amounts to is the claim that lexical sub-divisions imposed by lexical diacritics are respected except when they are not.

A more charitable interpretation of that claim would be that in majority of cases the combinatorics required by such diacritics is respected. The problem with the charitable interpretation is that it encourages the enshrining of an elite tendency as a principle of grammar, making a descriptive enterprise a normative exercise. The fact that most elite speakers most of the time respect combinatorics dictated by their sense of historical propriety needs to be stated but not at the level of system. It is best assigned to what might be called socio-morphology, which is at par with dictionary making.

Notice that we have deliberately side-lined the etymologically strict interpretation of such diacritics because their advocates have a ready-made answer to the objection that speakers don't know whether a given word is or is not of Latin, Sanskrit, or Persian origin. Their answer is that these labels do not correspond to, though they are based on, strict etymological inheritance. They claim that they merely sub-divide the lexicon into parts, some following this rule and others following that. Although this response seems to take care of cases like *preist-hood* by assigning *priest* to the sub-division Anglo-Saxon or Native, it is not clear what its empirical content is, for it seems to say only that there are words that end in *-hood* and words that end in *-ity*. Any set of competing word-formation strategies will automatically divide any given lexicon into as many sub-divisions as there are strategies in that set.

The question to ask is not what happens in a fully accessible given lexicon but what happens when the morphology extractable from that lexicon is called into play. What does a speaker do when he has, for example, forgotten a word or encounters a word his look-up procedure tells him is not in his lexicon? Even an elite speaker of English is perfectly capable of coming up with *ill-formity* as a noun correspondng to *ill-formed*, as is indirectly attested by the fact that he is perfectly capable of understanding the word if produced by another (elite or otherwise) speaker though he himself may have the word *ill-formedness* in his own mental lexicon.

The historically attested reflex of this is what has been called 'cross-over' above. The fact that it is not as commonly attested as it might be is easy to explain. Social filters of various sorts keep these 'mistakes' out of sight, even of the allegedly descriptive linguist. Notice that the term 'mistake' covers both what elite speakers may produce occasionally and what non-elite speakers produce fairly regularly. It is not an accident that varieties other than the standard are normally treated, even now, at least implicitly, as 'deviant'.

Morphological cross-over is not something to be neutralized or dismissed. It in fact raises the question: why isn't there more of it? Although we need to study the various institutional filters that keep it out of the records the linguist bases his discriptions on, there is no need to restrict its potentiality at the level of morphological competence, unless, of course, one wants to include fully articulated etymological competence of a hisotrical linguist in it. The 'escription that follows, therefore, dispenses with diacritics such as ± *tatsama*, ± Sanskrit and ± Perso-Arabic.

5.5 *On Not Deriving the Lexicon*

Recent developments in generative grammar, Fanselow (1988) correctly points out, make it necessary not only to adequately describe a linguistic regularity but also to identify the module (both within the 'mind' and within 'formal' competence) responsible for it. The fact that 'semantic' facts concerning scope or binding appear to be reducible to syntax and the fact that regularities in the domain of word-semantics appear to be consequences of general principles of our conceptual system (cf. Jackendoff 1983) suggest, according to Fanselow, that 'the organizational architecture of the human mind will not necessarily mirror the traditional partitioning of linguistics' (p.95). Phonology, the Lexicon, Morphology, Syntax, and Semantics, in other words, may have to be thought of somewhat differently.

One of the stable components of grammar has been the lexicon, though precisely what is in the lexicon has always presented serious empirical and conceptual problems, at least since Pāṇini's *-dhātupāṭh* (cf. Benson 1990). The earlier generative tradition, beginning with Lees (1960), held syntax responsible for its nonprimitives. Following Chomsky (1970), it was replaced by another tradition according to which the non-primitives were derived with the help of lexcion-specific word formation rules (cf. Halle 1973, Aronoff 1976 and Kiparsky 1982, amongst many others). This latter tradition finds itself faced with certain empirical problems, duly noted as early as Aronoff, that have led Pesetsky (1985) and Sproat (1985), for example, to propose some radical departures. The most radical of these is the proposal by Pesetsky that grammars may not contain a uniquely identifiable address traditionally referred to as the lexicon. This proposal, may not be warranted.

Chomsky's (1970) treatment of nominalizations in English has been, it should be obvious, interpreted in two ways. Amongst the adherents of what we shall call the weak interpretaion, Chomsky's demonstration is taken to mean, as Fanselow (1988) puts it, that the formation of complex words should not be accounted for by syntactic rules and principles. Those subscribing to what we shall call the strong interpretation take it to mean, as Bauer (1983:75) puts it, 'all nominalizations (and, by implication, all compounds and derivatives) are listed independently in the lexicon, i.e.they are treated as if they were fully lexicalized or simple lexemes'. It is the weak interpretation that allows Aronoff (1976) to see his word-based morphology, and Mohanan (1982) to see his lexical phonology and morphology, as not only consistent with but also as a consequence of Chomsky (1970). Jackendoff (1975) must, however, be seen as subscribing to the strong interpretation. In as much as they admit and allow the derivation of complex words by non-syntactic word-formation rules (WFR), most contemporary lexicalist versions of morphology clearly subscribe only to the weak interpretation. Partly becuse our view of syntax has changed considerably and partly because lexicalist models of morphology have had more than modest success, a return to the sort of position taken by Lees no longer seems possible.

One can, however, entertain the possibility of extending the mechanisms, rules and principles proposed for syntax beyond their usual sphere of application. According to Selkirk (1982), for example, the lexicon can be derived by extending the $\bar{X}$ schema 'below' syntax. Words, in other words, have an $\bar{X}$ - type syntax. Faced with 'bracketing paradoxes' of the sort that have become familiar in lexicalist models, Pesetsky argues for the application of both *Move* and binding theory in complex words and for the elimination of a uniquely identifiable locale in the grammar called the lexicon.

The $\bar{X}$ proposal, it is obvious, does not deny that there is a unique address 'lexicon' in the grammar; it merely says that it can, and perhaps should, be described in $\bar{X}$ terms. Given that non-head elements are generally not maximal projections below syntax, that word structure exhibits no interesting configurations comparable to specifier-adjunct-complement in syntax, and that the process of head-indentification in syntax and word-formation cannot be considered analogous (cf. Lieber 1980 and Fanselow 1988), it is difficult to accept the proposal that extends $\bar{X}$ 'below' syntax. Problems, however, remain for this weakly lexicalist theory of word-formation. Pesetsky and Sproat address these problems directly and argue for the integration of word-formation into syntax. Pesetsky also argues for the elimination of the lexicon as a separate, unique component, a bold move that deserves full attention and close scrutiny. His proposals deserve full attention because their logic seems compelling and close scrutiny because the lexicon as a component of grammar has rarely been challenged.

It should be obvious that Pesetsky's and Sproat's arguments are relevant only for the weak lexicalist position, the position that sees the lexicon as a joint set of underived, lexical primitives, some of which may be independently occurring words, and derived morphologically complex words. Whether the derivation of the latter involves only morphological operations of word-formation or phonological rules in addition to these is in principle irrelevant here. Although the weak lexicalist position assumes that the lexicon is derived by applying morphological and lexical phonological rules to underlying representations and that both the syntax and the phonology of words is different from phrasal syntax and phrasal phonology, it is not necessary to subscribe to the phrasal phonology word-phonology equation in order to maintain the weak lexicalist stance. A number of alternatives are possible, and some of them are examplified in studies such as Aronoff and Lieber. As what is common to all weak-lexicalist interpretations of the lexicon is the asumption that it is largely a product of WFRs, we shall not devote much attention to matters pertaining to what is generally referred to as lexical phonology.

The discussion above shows that the sorts of objections raised against the weak lexicalist position hinge crucially on the interpretation of morphology as a set of rules, subject to constraints such as 'Elsewhere and Level Ordering', that derive morphologically complex forms from morphologically simplex forms. They lose all their import if morphology were regarded as a set of generalized redundancy rules projected by or extracted from an underived lexicon, a lexicon consistent with the strong interpretation of Chomsky (1970). A strong lexicalist account of the lexicon does not view it as having been derived by WFRs: it views it as a stock of words a speaker can be legitimately said to possess. It views morphology as a system of rules that can be utilized to analyze known words should their analysis be needed or to generate words, fashioned after available ones, needed to meet specific needs such as having forgotten a word or having to coin one, etc. (cf.Ford and Singh 1992). This is the view we take in this book.

5.6 *On Exceptionality in Morphology*

According to Lakoff (1970), a theory of language should provide an evaluation measure that prefers grammars with few exceptions. That is, the grammar that points out the most regularities should be preferred. In terms of the only evaluation measures that have been proposed so far – those that map generality inversely into length – we would expect exceptions to count more than non-exceptional cases. Thus, all other things being equal, the grammar with the greater number of exceptions would have the greater length (Lakoff 1970:14).

Whereas recent developments in phonology and syntax seem to satisfy what might be called Lakoff's Preference (cited above), contemporary morphology still thrives on exceptionality and irregularity. This is particularly surprising because the lexicon has traditionally been supposed to be the repository of exceptions and if morphology captures the regularities in the lexicon, it is not clear what the status of exceptions to this storehouse of exceptions is or can be (cf. Singh, in press).

An adequate theory of morphology should minimize the need to have exceptions. This is in fact achieved in the theory espoused here for it builds on a generalized version of Jackendoff's (1975) redundancy rules and leaves suppletion out.

As we have seen, morphological relationship requires both formal and semantic similarity and is best captured by the rule-schema $[X]_{\alpha}$. $[X']_{\beta}$ where [X] and [X'] are words, "'" is the formal difference between X and X', and α and β are categories. This formulation, it should be obvious, provides a metalanguage for morphology that largely eliminates the need to have exceptions.

Some examples might be useful. Given morphological rules like the ones in (1) and (2), the need to have exceptions to plural formulation in French and German, for example, largely and perhaps even entirely disappears:

(1) a. $(X)_{n,\ sing} \longleftrightarrow (X)_{n,pl}$
    b. $(Xal)_{n,\ sing} \longleftrightarrow (Xo)_{n,pl}$

(2) a. $(X)_{n,\ sing} \longleftrightarrow (Xs)_{n,pl}$
    b. $(X)_{n,\ sing} \longleftrightarrow (Xa)_{n,pl}$
    c. $(X)_{n,\ sing} \longleftrightarrow (X)_{n,pl}$
    d. $(X)_{n,\ sing} \longleftrightarrow (Xs)_{n,pl}$

It is possible to ask: 'What empirical facts about word-formation does this sort of grammar account for, and, does the strong position lead to giving up any attempt to extract general principles of word-formation?' The central empirical fact this sort of grammar accounts for is that speakers do not coin words which their lexica do not license. As far as the other empirical 'facts' the generative tradition is replete with are concerned, they are better referred to, as Ford (personal communication) puts it, as *capta*. We do not, unfortunately, know of any empirical 'facts' substantial counter examples to which have not been pointed out within the generative tradition itself. After all, Pesetsky's proposal is an attempt to deal with facts that cannot be included within the 'empirical facts' now 'established' by the mini-tradition of lexical morphology (cf. Aronoff and Sridhar 1983). Although we are aware of the methodological import of this question, it is not necessarily to worry about *capta* taken to be 'facts' by this or that tradition. The full range of the facts of the matter is appropriately accounted for by grammars such as (1) and (2). Most of the allegedly empirical facts are dictionary-facts and not lexicon-facts. The distinction is important for the exercise of looking a word up is necessarily redundant.

One could also ask 'Are all rules in (1) and (2) of an equal status in the grammar, or are some less marked, say, than others?' Since it is not clear what 'marked' means (cf. Desrochers 1990), all one can say is that 'potentially 'yes', 'but' 'actually no' because their application is constrained by processing and frequency considerations and that when such considerations are not involved there is no way to predict which option will be taken. The structural complexity of a rule is a transparent enough index of its actualization potential and when two rules have the same complexity and frequency pull one is as likely to apply as the other, apparently the case with German plurals listed in (2), despite the pedagogical emphasis on one of them (cf. Phillips and Bouma 1980).

Groups of words that exhibit no formal similarity or constitute unique pairs are examples of suppletion, something outside morphology, and not of exceptions to anything.

One could argue that we are eliminating exceptions by stipulating that they be eliminated and bring up what one sees as the 'morphological relationship' between English *go* and *went*. Now, *go* and *went* are undoubtedly related but what that relationship has to do with morphology escapes us. Morphology is that sub-type of lexical relatedness which requires both semantic and formal relationship. The lack of former rules out morphological relatedness in the case of English adjective /red / and past tense verbal /red / and the lack of latter rules it out in the case of *go* and *went*. Examples like *kill* and *murder* and *good* and *well* show that, contrary to text-book assumptions, suppletion, even in its strong form, is not unknown outside 'inflection'. The definition of morphology that includes the former but excludes the latter remains incomprehensible to us despite its very respectable ancestry. The point here is that we are not ruling out what is generally called suppletion in order to eliminate exceptions but that what appears to be the proper conceptualization of morphology does not allow its inclusion. It is, of course, possible to disagree with that conceptualization, as most Pāṇinians, including Bloomfield and his successors like Halle, do.

Chapter 6

MODERN HINDI: SOME ANALYTICAL PRELIMINARIES

6.0 *Introduction*

As the description that follows in Chapter 8 may appear unfamiliar to some readers, it will be useful to spell out in some detail some of the conceptual and organizational issues involved in that description. How radical a particular conceptual or organizational decision appears to be is, of course, a function of what the reader's own mental baggage is. A reader accustomed to regarding *ne* in MH as an ergative case marker or as a *kartā kārak* would be surprised, for example, to find that our description does not refer to it as a word-part anywhere. We regard it as a postposition and not as a *vibhakti* which, for us, must be morphologically bound. What follows is a description of MH lexical items or of MH departures from Sanskrit. It is a description of that part of lexical relatedness that meets, we repeat, the joint requirements of formal and semantic relatedness. It is, in other words, a description of whatever can be legitimately said to be going on amongst morphologically related words. This is not to deny that there are relationships between the postpositional head and the noun that it governs or between the auxiliary and the verb, but simply to state that these relationships fall outside the domain of morphology. Inter-word relationships in various kinds of phrases are important but irrelevant here. Also irrelevant are paraphrastic expressions of whatever notional or semantic categories grammarians have traditionally chosen to talk about. The fact that "futurity" can, as it must, be expressed in English, as in any other language, does not, for example, entitle one to claim that English has 'future tense', certainly not in the sense in which, for example Latin and Sanskrit do. The grouping of *Ved* with *will V* in English may have some pedagogical utility but is certainly of no consequence morphologically.

6.1 *Invariable Words*

A substantial chunk of Hindi lexical stock consists of words that do not change their form in any context except when, in some cases, they are reduplicated. Some of these invariant words may appear to be morphologically complex themselves. Irrespective of their putative morphological complexity, these words do not participate in any word-formation processes except in reduplication (which is beyond the scope of this book). They do not show any changes in relation to person, number, gender, tense, aspect etc. These words have to be learnt, and no morphological strategy can aid their acquisition.

For example, Hindi adverbs are generally invariant. Words like *jəldi* 'quickly'; *dhire* 'slowly'; *age* 'in front of'; *əb* 'now'; *ɪslɪye* 'therefore' etc. do not undergo any change whatever be the syntactic context in which they are used (except, as pointed out above, in reduplication).

Adverbs of time e.g. *kəl* 'yesterday/tomorrow'; *axɪr* 'finally'; *pərsõ* 'day after tomorrow'; *jəb* 'when'; *roz* 'daily'; *ekdəm* 'suddenly'; *phɪr* 'again'; *əksər* 'often' etc. are all invariable. Adverbs of frequency e.g. *barbar* 'again and again'; *bəhʊdha* 'generally'; *hərbar* 'every time'; *hərghəṛi* 'every moment' etc. are also invariant though some of them are morphologically complex. Similarly adverbs of place e.g. *pas* 'near'; *kəhã* 'where'; *vəhã* 'there'; *upər* 'above'; *nice* 'below'; *samne* 'in front of'; *piche* 'behind'; *dur* 'far'; *aspas* 'on all sides' and adverbs of direction e.g. *ɪdhər* 'this side'; *ʊdhər* 'that side '; *kɪdhər* 'which side'; etc. are all invariant, again, irrespective of their own morphological complexity.

Adverbs of manner e.g. *əcanək* 'suddenly'; *səcmʊc* 'truely'; *vyərth* 'in vain'; *šayəd* 'perhaps'; *dhyānpurvək* 'carefully'; *səhəj* 'easily'; *phəṭaphəṭ* 'quickly' and adverbs of degree e.g. *ləgbhəg* 'approximately'; *bɪlkʊl* 'completely'; *purṇtəya* 'completely'; *bərabər* 'equally' etc. are all invariant. To this we may add adverbs of affirmation and negation e.g. *na* 'no'; *hã* 'yes'; *ji* 'polite yes'; *mət* 'do not'.

The postpositions e.g. *ne, ko, se, mẽ* and *pər* are invariable. The only postposition which changes form according to the number and gender of the following noun is *ka* 'of'. All conjunctions, including the coordinators *ɔr/və/evəm/təthа* 'and'; disjunctives *ya/va/əthva* 'or' and adversative conjunctions *pər/pərəntu/kɪntʊ/ məgər/lekɪn* 'but' are also invariable.

All interjections whether expressing joy e.g. *aha, ha, vah-vah* or sorrow e.g. *hay, əha. ah. ɔf, əfsos* or surprise e.g. *əre , kya* or applause e.g. *šabaš, khub* etc. remain unchanged.

6.2 *Pronouns*

Another category of words which, though its members can be said to be related, does not call for the postulation of WFSs consists of the

Hindi pronouns. Though pronouns in MH (see below) show number and case differences, they constitute a finite set. Since the strategies relating them cannot be invoked to create new forms, it will indeed be pointless to formulate these strategies. This restriction, it is important to emphasize, follows from the limits of the pronominal system and not from those of the putative WFSs. Hindi has the following personal pronouns:

Person	*Sing*	*Pl*	*Obl Sing*	*Obl Pl*
I	mæ̃	həm	mæ̃ne, mujhe,	həmẽ.
	I	we	mera/meri	həmara/həmari
II	tum	tum (log)		tumhẽ
	you	you (people)		tumhara/tumhari
	tu	tujhe		
	you (non-hon)			
	ap	ap (log)		
	you (hon)	you people		
III	vəh	ve	unhẽ	
	he/she	they	unko	

The second person (non-hon) *tu* 'you' is used in situations of extreme respect, affection, intimacy, anger or disrespect. It should be used for gods, mother, friends, enemies or servants. *tum* is relatively neutral with respect to politeness and is often used among equals reciprocally. *ap* denotes politeness and respect.

The four demonstrative pronouns, used to indicate nearness or distance are *yəh* 'this', *ye* 'these'; *vəh* 'that'; *ve* 'those'. The five reflexive pronouns *ap, əpna, əpne, əpne-ap. svəyəm/khud* always refer to the logical subject of the sentence. Notice that the reflexive *ap* can refer to any 'person' whereas the second person honorific *ap* is simply polite 'you'.

The only relative pronoun Hindi has is *jo* 'who, which, that, what'; *so* 'he, they' as a correlative of *jo* is now rarely used.

The two indefinite pronouns of Hindi include *koi* 'somebody'; *kuch* 'something'.

The two interrogative pronouns are *kɔn* 'who'; *kya* 'what'.

The total number of pronouns in Hindi is thus 44 or so. They are either not related to each other or are related in idiosyncratic ways. They will have to be listed as such in a speaker's lexicon. They, in general, do not involve the application of any WFS. Even if some could be postulated, their guaranteed non-application—the pronominal system cannot be extended at will would make such an exercise pointless.

We will, therefore, have nothing more to say about pronouns or invariant words.

6.3 *Tense and Aspect*

Another conceptual issue that we would like to clarify concerns the marking of tense and aspect in the Hindi verb. This is again an area where the desire to discover traditional grammatical categories has resulted in avoidable complexity and confusion. If we appreciate the fact that the auxiliary in Hindi is a finite set of formally unrelated words (and therefore simply need to be listed and memorized) and the main verb is a part of regular and productive word-formation processes (and therefore forms an essential component of the morphological description of Hindi), several things will fall into place. Without any loss of any significant generalization, our description will look fairly straightforward and elegant.

Tense is really a matter of locating an event in time, present, past or future. Sometimes a given event may have to be located simultaneously in terms of two or more time-reference points. Aspect is a matter of how the speaker views the nature of the event to be located in time e.g. not yet begun, complete, incomplete, contingent or continuous. Most Hindi grammarians have analyzed the Hindi verbal system simultaneously in terms of tense (present, past and future) and aspect (perfect and imperfect) isolating *linguistic expressions* that correlate with different combinations of tense and aspect.

Though simplified in comparison to Ethrington (1871) and Kellogg's (1876) tables, the following table from Guru (1920:261) is typical. Guru defines tense as the verbal form which marks both the time and nature of a given event.

Ordinary	*Imperfect*	*Perfect*	
Present	-ta hæ	-rəha/hæ	-a hæ
Past	-a	-ta tha	
	rəha/tha	-a tha	
Future	-ega		

It is clear that except *-ega* of the future, no morphological ending in the main verb is *uniquely* associated with a tense-aspect distinction. *-ta* ending could appear either in the present or the past (or as a present participle). What really distinguishes the ordinary present from the past imperfect is the auxiliary *hæ* in the first case and *tha* in the second. Similarly, the present perfect is distinguished from the past perfect not by the *-a* ending in the main verb but by the presence of the different forms of the auxiliaries. The progressive marker *rəha* is an independent word anyway, associated perhaps with the verb *rəha* 'lived'. Here also the tense distinction between the present and the past is carried by the auxiliary and *not* by the main verb or even the progressive marker.

We may therefore conclude that tense, with the exception of the future tense, is marked only in the auxiliary. Notice that *-ta* is not uniquely associated with presentness:

vəh cəlta hæ	'he walks'
vəh cəlta tha	'he used to walk'
vəh cəlta ho	'If we were walking'
vəh cəlta hota	'he may be walking'
vəh cəlta hoga	'he must be walking'
cəlta hua ləɽka	'walking boy'

Similarly, *-a* is not uniquely associated with pastness:

vəh cəla	'he walked'
vəh cəla hæ	'he has walked'
vəh cəla tha	'he had walked'
vəh cəla ho	'he may have walked'
vəh cəla hota	'if he had walked'
vəh cəla hoga	'he must have walked'
cəla hua ləɽka	'boy who has walked'

If we carefully examine the tense and aspect Tables of Ethrington (1871) and Kellogg (1876), we realise that, there are no morphologically unique correlates of tense and aspect distinctions in the main verb. *-ta* ending is used for both simple present and past indefinite. Both these tenses use the *-ta* ending in the main verb. The burden of distinguishing these tenses is really carried by the auxiliary *hæ* 'be'. The other changes in the *-ta* suffix really mark person, number and gender changes, and not the tense or aspect differences. Similarly, no morphological marking in the main verb separates the simple past, present perfect and past perfect. The main verb actually appears in its participle form with (carrying) the past participle marker. Kellogg's Table, in fact, makes it clear that the only real distinction to be made in the main verb morphology is between the root, the imperfect *-ta* participle and the perfect *-a* participle. The very appearance of the participle form gives away the compound or periphrastic nature of tense in Modern Hindi.

Morphologically, we believe, a word-formation strategy of *-ta* adjunction forming the imperfect aspect or imperfect participle is bidirectionally related to, among other things, the second person singular imperative e.g. *cəl* 'walk' and it is this form which combines with the different forms of the auxiliary to obtain tense and/or aspect distinctions. Similarly, it is strategy of *-a* adjunction to the main verb that forms the perfect participle or mark the perfective aspect which *when* combined with various forms of the auxiliary expresses not only simple past, but also the present and past perfect, the contingent perfect, presumptive perfect and past contingent perfect. Notice that the participle forming word-parts *-ta* and *-a* are affixed to a word (and not to a base form or a *dhātu*). Periphrastic expressions of tense-aspect distinctions fall outside the domain of morphology.

If we accept Vajpeyi's (1958) proposal that *ga* be accepted as the future auxiliary on the analogy of the present *hæ* and past *tha*, Hindi will actually have no verbal tense. However that proposal is unacceptable for reasons given in Srivastava (1990).

The confusion created by not defining the domain of morphology rigorously is seen most clearly when we compare, for example, Platts (1873) and Guru (1920). Platts posits nine tense-aspect distinctions (3 simple and 6 complex) whereas Guru posits sixteen (6 simple and 10 complex). The Fig 6.1 displays these categories. The classification made by Platts has been put in brackets.

We maintain that the morphologically simple imperative verb form. is bidirectionally related to the morphologically complex verbal forms through adjunction involving the word-parts *-e* (contingent mood), *-ta* (imperfect aspect), *-a* (perfect aspect), *-na* (infinitive) and *-ega* (future tense). Schematically, Hindi verbal m orphology may be represented as:

Fig. 6.1 Tense-Aspect distinctions in Platts (1873) and Guru (1920)
(Platts' classification is shown in brackets)

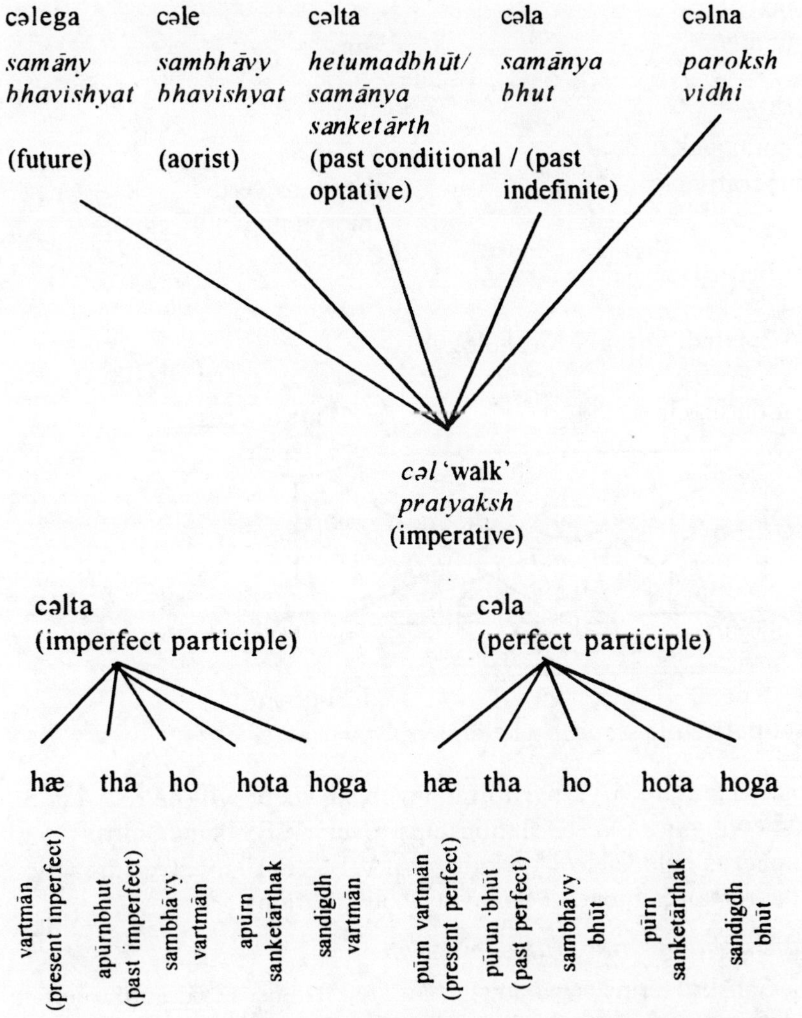

As a matter of fact, we need to make only the following distinctions in the verbal morphology of Hindi:

(a) *Tense*	*Main Verb*	*Auxiliary*
Present	-	he
Past	-	tha
Future	-ega	

(b) *Aspect*

Imperfect	-ta
Perfect	-a
Infinitival	-na

(c) *Mood*

Contingent	-e
Imperative	the main verb (morphologically simple word)

Fig 6.2: Hindi Verbal Morphology

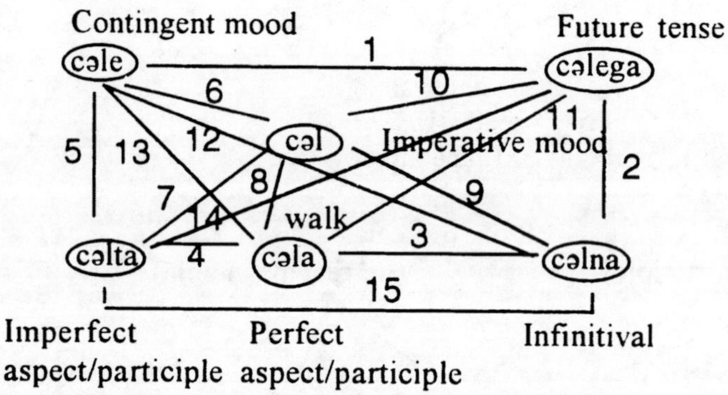

Since there are 6 verbal forms involved, there will be 6x5 i.e. 30 WFSs showing intra-verb relationships. Every WFS being bidirectional this number is reduced to 15. Notice that WFSs 6-10 involve adjunction while the remaining ten WFSs involve substitutions.

6.4 *Guṇa, Vṛddhi and Glide-Insertion*

The Sanskrit terms *guṇa* and *vṛddhi* are often used to describe certain morphophonemic changes that take place in WFSs. *guṇa* implies prefixing *a-* to a simple vowel, while *vṛddhi* involves further *a-* prefixation to a *guṇa* vowel. Thus *guṇa* changes *i* to *e* and *u* to *o* as in intranstitive/transitive pairs *mɪl, mel; dɪkh, dekh; tʊl, tol; khʊl, khol* etc.

However, *guṇa* is not an across the board phonological process in modern Hindi. In comparable pairs, we get *lʊṭ* (and not **loṭ*); *bhʊn, bhun* (and not *bhon).

Glide insertion between two vowels is also often invoked to explain morphophonemic changes which are actually tied to sets of words that form the basis of WFSs involving these changes. For example, there are two ways in which we could represent the morphological relationship obtaining between pairs e.g.

kha,. khaya; pi, piya; so, soya

We could represent it in terms of an adjunction strategy

(1) $(X)_{v} \longleftrightarrow (Xya)_{v,\ perf/pt\ parti}$

or we could obtain these forms from the WFS (2) invoking glide insertion:

(2) $(X)_{v} \longleftrightarrow (Xa)_{v,\ pt/pt\ parti}$

WFS (2) also produces the following pairs in which X ends in a C:

cəl. cəla: mər, məra; bhag, bhaga

WFS (2) may also be considered sufficient to produce pairs in which X ends in a V if we add the rule: if X ends in V, add a glide before *-a* adjunction. However it will not be a legitimate solution. We could invoke glide insertion if it were an across the board phonological rule and sequences e.g. XVV were not allowed in Hindi. But such sequences are very common as in

soi, khoi, gehʊa, boi, bʊa etc.

So, we need two WFSs – one for consonant-ending words and the other for vowel-ending words – to indicate morphological relationship that obtains between the perfective aspect or past participles and imperative verbs. In WFS (1), X ends in V and in WFS (2) X ends in a C.

CHAPTER 7

SOME ORGANIZATIONAL MATTERS

7.0 *Introduction*

This chapter describes the way in which morphological relations obtaining among the major grammatical categories of MH (Noun, Verb, Adjective and Adverb) are organized. Sections A, B, C and D deal with Nominal Morphology i.e. with Word Formation Strategies obtaining between Nouns and Nouns (A), Nouns and Verbs (B), Nouns and Adjectives (C) and Nouns and Adverbs (D); E, F and G deal with Verbal Morphology; H and I with Adjectival and J with Adverbial Morphology. Since the morphological relations obtaining between Verbs and Nouns (B') are the same as between Verbs and Nouns (B) and so on for all the empty slots below, we do not need to duplicate our work.

	Nouns	*Verbs*	*Adjectives*	*Adverbs*
Noun	A	B	C	D
Verb	(B')	E	F	G
Adjective	(C')	(F')	H	I
Adverb	(D')	(G')	(I')	J

7.1 *Conventions Used*

Each WFS subsumes both a formal and a semantic relation. Further, we posit a WFS only if there are two or more instances of its application. The pair

put	kəput
son	bad son

appears to be related both formally and semantically. But this is the only pair available at the moment, though both the words are used very frequently. The initial *kə-* of

kəgar 'precipice'; *kəcra* 'rubbish': *kəṭar* 'dagger'

though formally identical has no semantic similarity with *kə-* of *kəput*. We may best characterise the relationship in question as follows:

$$(\text{put})_{\text{n, nom, masc, sing}} \longleftrightarrow (\text{kəput})_{\text{n, nom, masc, sing}}$$

as a dormant strategy which may get activated at a later stage. It is also possible that *kəput* like *kəʈar* etc. is seen as morphologically simple and is in fact never analysed by a majority of speakers.

The distinction between a WFS and a Dormant Strategy (DS) is essentially a matter of whether there are sufficient grounds for the speaker to analyse a string as made up of a word plus some specified material. We believe more than one instance of some relation is needed for the licence to postulate the abstraction of variables. Deliberate exploitation of paradigmatic minimality is, of course, possible and happens all the time, with predictable consequences—amusement or disapproval. It is perhaps more desirable to leave a solitary relationship, like the one between *put* and *kəput* for most speakers, alone as unformulated, implying that it is not analyzed. The putative morphological simplicity of *kəput* will follow directly from the absense of such an analysis. Such strategies are listed as Dormant Strategies (DS) in 8.11.

Other conventions used in the description are:

1. Material within the parenthesis is always a word.
2. Variable X is used to designate words. Letters P,Q,R etc. are used to designate parts of words that are longer than one segment, They do not, it is important to point out, count as variables in the same sense in which X is a variable (cf. Chapter 3).
3. Unless covered by the Heuristic Devices in 7.2 all WFSs are fully and redundantly specified in terms of values of different features. Thus, specification for the feature case subsumes that the word involved is a noun yet the major grammatical category value 'n' is given any way.
4. All WFSs are bidirectional and could be activated in either direction.
5. Each WFS is followed by two examples with glosses. There are, of course, generally many more examples for each WFS.
6. In general, the features that change are mentioned towards the end of the feature-matrix.

7. A slash is used when a WFS holds good for more than one but not all values of a given feature or a feature-complex.
8. Each feature-value is separated by a comma. A comma is not used when a bundle of feature-values is used to designate a form.
9. Though in principle, complex word-parts are as easily accessible as simple word-parts, we opt for a description which restricts itself to simple word-parts only. Thus to get *jadugərnıyõ* 'female magicians' (obl), though the speaker will have a direct access to *-gərnıyõ* as in.

$(X)_{n,\ masc,\ sing,\ nom} \longleftrightarrow (Xg\text{ə}rn\text{ı}y\tilde{o})_{n,\ fem,\ pl,\ obl}$

we represent it as

(X) ⟷ (Xgər)
↓
(X) ⟷ (Xni)
↓
(Xi) ⟷ (Xıyõ)

It is a descriptive device. No theoretical import should be attached to this decision.

7.2 *Heuristic Devices (HD)*

The number of WFSs that need to be explicitly stated can be reduced by using some Heuristic Devices (HD). We suppress these predictable strategies not for reasons of 'economy'(in the standard sense) but for reasons of economics (cost of paper and printing). We affirm the existence of these predictable strategies in all mental lexica, the only kind of lexica we recognize the existence of. No theoretical import should be attributed to this vulgar economic decision of ours.

HDI: *Underspecification*

If an X remains invariant across different values (e.g. nom, obl and voc) of a given feature (e.g. case), then it is left unspecified for that feature in the WFSs in which it participates. Thus, underspecification for case, as we will see below, will help us to collapse three strategies into one. It is of course assumed by the theory that all the three WFSs exist in the mental lexica

HD II: *Identity*

If an X is involved in a set of WFSs involving identity and if the same X is also involved in another WFS involving adjunction, substitution etc., then the latter WFS is stated only once though it is clear that it is automatically and inevitably related to each WFS in the former set involving identity relationships.

HD III: *Substitution*

If β can be attached to a variable of the type X or P to which α can also be attached, then a substitution strategy of the type

$$(X\alpha) \longleftrightarrow (X\beta)$$

follows automatically; and vice versa.

HD IV: *Feature Matrix Identity*

Given a set of related words, if there is a WFS $(X)_\alpha \longleftrightarrow (X)_\beta$ and there is also a WFS $(X)_\alpha \longleftrightarrow (X)_\gamma$, where $_{\alpha,\ \beta}$ and $_\gamma$ are feature matrices, then $(X)_\alpha \longleftrightarrow (X)_\gamma$ follows.

Consider now sub-sets of related words in the case of *sunar* 'goldsmith' and *nag* 'snake':

sʊnar, sʊnarõ, sʊnaro, sʊnarin,
nag, nagõ, nago, nagɪn

A fully redundant and explicitly stated description of the WFSs in which these words participate is given below:

1. $(X)_{\text{n, masc, sing, nom}} \longleftrightarrow (X)_{\text{n, masc sing, obl}}$
2. $(X)_{\text{n, masc,sing, nom}} \longleftrightarrow (X)_{\text{n, masc, sing, voc}}$
3. $(X)_{\text{n, masc, sing, obl}} \longleftrightarrow (X)_{\text{n, masc, sing, voc}}$
4. $(X)_{\text{n, masc, nom, sing}} \longleftrightarrow (X)_{\text{n, masc, nom, pl}}$

5. $(X)_{\text{n, masc, obl, sing}} \longleftrightarrow (X)_{\text{n, masc, nom, pl}}$

6. $(X)_{\text{n, masc, vol, sing}} \longleftrightarrow (X)_{\text{n, masc, nom, pl}}$

7. $(X)_{\text{n, masc, nom, sing}} \longleftrightarrow (X\tilde{o})_{\text{n, masc, obl, pl}}$

8. $(X)_{\text{n, masc, obl, sing}} \longleftrightarrow (X\tilde{o})_{\text{n, masc, obl, pl}}$

9. $(X)_{\text{n, masc, voc, sing}} \longleftrightarrow (X\tilde{o})_{\text{n, masc, obl, pl}}$

10. $(X)_{\text{n, masc, nom, pl}} \longleftrightarrow (X\tilde{o})_{\text{n, masc, obl, pl}}$

11. $(X)_{\text{n, masc, nom, sing}} \longleftrightarrow (Xo)_{\text{n, masc, voc, pl}}$

12. $(X)_{\text{n, masc, obl, sing}} \longleftrightarrow (Xo)_{\text{n, masc, voc, pl}}$

13. $(X)_{\text{n, masc, voc, sing}} \longleftrightarrow (Xo)_{\text{n, masc, voc, pl}}$

14. $(X)_{\text{n, masc, nom, pl}} \longleftrightarrow (Xo)_{\text{n, masc, voc, pl}}$

15. $(X)_{\text{n, nom, sing, masc}} \longleftrightarrow (X\text{ɪn})_{\text{n, nom, sing, fem}}$

16. $(X)_{\text{n, obl, sing, masc}} \longleftrightarrow (X\text{ɪn})_{\text{n, nom, sing, fem}}$

17. $(X)_{\text{n, voc, sing, masc}} \longleftrightarrow (X\text{ɪn})_{\text{n, nom, sing, fem}}$

18. $(X)_{\text{n, nom, pl, masc}} \longleftrightarrow (X\text{ɪn})_{\text{n, nom, sing, fem}}$

19. $(X\tilde{o})_{\text{n, masc, obl, pl}} \longleftrightarrow (Xo)_{\text{n, masc, voc, pl}}$

20. $(X\tilde{o})_{\text{n, masc, obl, pl}} \longleftrightarrow (X\text{ɪn})_{\text{n, nom, sing, fem}}$

21. $(Xo)_{\text{n, masc, voc, pl}} \longleftrightarrow (X\text{ɪn})_{\text{n, nom, sing, fem}}$

Essentially we are dealing with 7 forms of *sɪnar* or *nag*, 4 of which are phonologically identical. For *sɪnar*, we have

(a) sunar	:	nom, sing, masc
(b) sunar	:	obl, sing, masc
(c) sunar	:	voc, sing, masc
(d) sunar	:	nom, pl, masc
(e) sunarõ	:	obl, pl, masc
(f) sunaro	:	voc, pl, masc
(g) sunarın	:	nom, sing, fem

Given these 7 forms, we can have 7x6=42 WFSs relating them to each other. The principle of bidirectionality helps us reduce these WFSs to the 21 stated above. The heuristic devices we have proposed will help us to further reduce the number of WFSs that need to be explicitly stated.

If we apply HD I involving underspecification to WFSs 7-9 above, we get 7' subsuming WFSs 7-9:

7' $(X)_{\text{n, masc, sing}} \longleftrightarrow (X\tilde{o})_{\text{n, masc, obl, pl}}$

Similarly WFSs 11-13 are automatically subsumed in 11'.

11' $(X)_{\text{n, masc, sing}} \longleftrightarrow (Xo)_{\text{n, masc, voc, pl}}$

HD I thus reduces 6 WFSs to 2. Consider now the WFSs 15-18. The LHS of these WFSs is involved in an already stated set of WFSs(1-6) involving identity. We can therefore use HD II. Thus

15' $(X)_{\text{n, masc, sing}} \longleftrightarrow (X\text{ın})_{\text{n, masc, sing, fem}}$

subsumes that (Xın) could be accessed through all the four identical Xs (a-d above).

If we implement HD III, we do not need to state 19, 20 and 21 at all. These substitution relationships are subsumed under earlier WFSs where *-õ*, *-o*, and *-ın* are suffixed to the same X.

The principle of bidirectionality and the three heuristic devices help us to reduce the description from 42 to 11 WFSs. Given the exponential nature of the way word-formation strategies seem to multiply, these are obviously useful descriptive devices. We insist that a native speaker must actually possess these 42 WFSs for these words (which will of course multiply exponentially as they plug into other similar networks e.g. that of *sunarm*) and that these must be assumed to exist as they are recoverable from the implementation of the principle of bidirectionality and the three heuristic devices.

The fact that the heuristics above eliminate the need to explicitly write the strategy that relates PQ $\longleftrightarrow$ PR, may lead one to think that this device renders our description equivalent to the description in which (PQ) and (PR) are derived from (P) by the adjunction of Q and R. That this is not the case should be obvious from the fact that P has no status in the theory which guides this description — only $(PQ)_{\alpha}$ and $(PR)_{\beta}$ do. "Derivations" like the following are not possible in this theory

nomin → $(\text{nominate})_{\text{verb}}$

nomin → $(\text{nominee})_{\text{noun}}$

The only relationship allowed is between *nominate* and *nominee* and as we pointed out earlier, it is mediated by substitution:

$$(\text{Pate})_{v} \longleftrightarrow (\text{Pee})_{n}$$

Notice that the (P) above has no status independent of the *-ate* or the *-ee* with which it appears in *nominate* and *nominee*.

Or, to take the example of *pətəŋ, pətəŋõ, pətəŋbaz* the heuristic suppression of

$$[\text{Xõ}]_{\text{n, obl, pl}} \longleftrightarrow [\text{Xbaz}]_{\text{n, nom, sing}}$$

does not entail 'derivational path' of the following sort:

pətəŋ → pətəŋbaz

pətəŋ → pətəŋõ

The relationship between *pətəŋõ* and *pətəŋbaz* is straightforward and automatic, though left unstated for reasons of "heuristic economy". This sort of economy should not be confused with neo-Paṇinian economy, which is an economy of derivational paths. Single bridge-heads provide shortest derivational paths in that theory, forcing the postulation of abstract, ontologically unmotivated and dubious entities. The alleged "root" *nomin* is thus an artefact of the refusal to recognise the direct relationship between *nominate* and *nominee*.

It is worth repeating that the shortest path theory fails to capture certain crucial facts. Although it is fine to say that *adverbiaux* and *adverbial* in French are related via the bridge-head *adverb*, it is not clear how the shortest path theory can even express the fact that for every plural that ends in *-aux* in French there is a singular that ends in *-al*. The dependence of *-aux* "attachment" on *"-al"* becomes a curious fact in this theory, for *-aux* should be able to go its own way.

We'd be willing to charitably assume that standard neo-Pāṇinian descriptions had this implicit relationship in mind were it not the case that they insist on its not being there, that they postulate units other than words as possible domains for morphological operations and offer no explanation for the mutual dependency of, for example, *-al* and *-aux* in French and *-ate* and *-ee* in English.

CHAPTER 8

HINDI WORD FORMATION STRATEGIES

8.0 *Introduction*

This chapter lists the WFSs that capture the relationships obtaining in different sets of morphologically related words. It is important to keep in mind the conventions and heuristic devices listed in Chapter 7 to fully understand the WFSs listed below. Though we have made every possible attempt to make the description as comprehensive as possible, we may have unwittingly left out some WFSs. A revised version will of course incorporate all the suggestions we receive.

8.1 *Nouns and Nouns* (A)

(a) Identity (WFSs 1-7)

1. $(X)_{\text{n. sing. nom}} \longleftrightarrow (X)_{\text{n. sing. obl}}$

Condition: X is not a masculine noun ending in -a unless it is a honorific word e.g. *dada* 'grandfather'

ghər	ghər (masc)
'house'	'house'
lerki	lerki (fem)
'girl'	'girl'

2. $(X)_{\text{n. sing. nom}} \longleftrightarrow (X)_{\text{n. sing. voc}}$

Condition: X is not a masculine noun ending in -a unless it is a honorific word e.g. *dada* 'grandfather'

admi	admi (masc)
'man'	'O man!'
rajkumari	rajkumari (fem)
'princess'	'O princess!'

3. $(X)_{\text{n. nom. masc. sing}} \longleftrightarrow (X)_{\text{n. nom. masc. pl}}$

Condition: X does not end in -a unless it is a honorific word
e.g. *dada* 'grandfather'

sənduk	sənduk
'box'	'boxes'
admi	admi
'man'	'men'

4. $(X)_{\text{n. masc. obl. sing}} \longleftrightarrow (X)_{\text{n. masc. nom. pl}}$

Condition: X does not end in -a unless it is a honorific word
e.g. *dada* 'grandfather'

mez	mez
'table'	'tables'
sənduk	sənduk
'box'	'boxes'

5. $(X)_{\text{n. masc. voc. sing}} \longleftrightarrow (X)_{\text{n. masc. nom. pl}}$

Condition: X does not end in -a unless it is a honorific word.

admi	admi
'O man!'	'men'
ghər	ghər
'O house!'	'houses'

6. $(X)_{\text{n. masc. obl. sing}} \longleftrightarrow (X)_{\text{n. masc. nom. pl}}$

Condition : X ends in -e.

ləɽke	ləɽke
'boy'	'boys'
ghoɽe	ghoɽe
'horse'	'horses'

7. $(X)_{\text{n. masc. voc. sing}} \longleftrightarrow (X)_{\text{n. masc. nom. pl}}$

Condition : X ends in -e.

dərvaze	dərvaze
'O door!'	'doors'
ghoɽe	ghoɽe
'O horse!'	'horses'

(b) *Suffixation* (WFSs 8-53)

8. $(X)_{\text{n. masc. sing. inani}} \longleftrightarrow (Xi)_{\text{n. masc.sing.}}$ *one who deals in* X

Condition: X ends in a consonant.

tel	teli
'oil'	'one who deals in oil'
kəbaɽ	kəbaɽi
'garbage'	'one who deals in garbage'

9. $(X)_{\text{n. masc. sing. abs}} \longleftrightarrow (Xi)_{\text{n. masc. sing.}}$ *one who practices* X

Condition: X ends in a consonant.

əpradh	əpradhi
'crime'	'criminal'
sənyas	sənyasi
'renunciation'	'saint'

10. $(X)_{\text{n. masc. sing. nom. pl. inani}} \longleftrightarrow (Xi)_{\text{n. masc. sing.}}$ *hailing from* X

Condition : X ends in a consonant.

pəhaɽ	pəhaɽi
'hills'	'from the hills'
dehat	dehati
'rural area'	'from the rural area'

11. $(X)_{n,\ sing,\ nom,\ pl,\ masc,\ hum} \longleftrightarrow (Xi)_{n,\ sing,\ fem,}$ *abs* X

Condition : X ends in a consonant.

dost	dosti
'friend'	'friendship'
dušmən	dušməni
'enemy'	'enemity'

12. $(X)_{n,\ sing,\ nom,\ pl,\ hum,\ masc} \longleftrightarrow (Xi)_{n,\ sing,\ hum,\ fem}$

Condition: X ends in a consonant.

das	dasi
'servant'	'maid'
rajkumar	rajkumari
'prince'	'princess'

13. $(X)_{n,\ fem,\ sing} \longleftrightarrow (X\tilde{e})_{n,\ fem,\ pl,\ nom}$

Condition: X does not end in -i, -ɪ or -u.

rat	ratẽ
'night'	'nights'
mala	malaẽ
'garland'	'garlands'

14. $(X)_{n,\ sing/nom\ pl,\ masc} \longleftrightarrow (Xa)_{n,\ sing,\ hum,\ fem}$

Condition: X ends in a consonant.

chatr	chatra
'student'	'female student'
valɪd	valɪda
'father'	'mother'

15. $(X)_{n.\ sing} \longleftrightarrow (Xo)_{n.\ voc,\ pl}$

Condition: X does not end in -ɪ, -i, or -u. It also does not end in -a if X is masculine, honorific words excluded.

ghər	ghəro (masc)
'house'	'O houses!'
mala	malao (fem)
'garland'	'O garlands!'
vəstʊ	vəstʊo
'thing'	'O things!' (masc)
raja	rajao (masc, hon)
'king'	'O kings!'

16. $(X)_{n.\ masc,\ pl,\ nom} \longleftrightarrow (Xo)_{n.\ masc,\ pl,\ voc}$

Condition: X does not end in -ɪ, -i, or -u. It also does not end in -a, unless it is an honorific word.

sənduk	sənduko
'boxes'	'O boxes!'
šɪšʊ	śɪšʊo
'children'	'O children!'
raja	rajao
'kings'	'O kings!'

17. $(X)_{n.\ sing} \longleftrightarrow (X\tilde{o})_{n.\ obl,\ pl}$

Condition: X does not end in -ɪ, -i, or -u. It also does not end in -a if X is masculine, honorific words excluded.

rat	ratõ (fem)
'night'	'nights'
sənduk	səndukõ (masc)
'box'	'boxes'
vəstʊ	vəstʊõ (fem)
'thing'	'things'
dada	dadaõ (masc, hon)
'grandfather'	'grandfathers'

18. $(X)_{n,\ masc,\ pl,\ nom,}$ ⟷ $(X\tilde{o})_{n,\ masc,\ pl,\ obl}$

Condition: X does not end in -ɪ, -i or -u. It also does not end in -a, unless it is an honorific word.

məkan	məkanõ
'houses'	'houses'
šɪšu	šɪšuõ
'children'	'children'
nana	nanaõ
'maternal grandfather'	'maternal grandfathers'

19. $(X)_{n,\ sing,\ hum,\ fem}$ ⟷ $(Xoi)_{n,\ sing,\ hum,\ masc,}$ *X's husband*

bəhɪn	bəhɪnoi
'sister'	'sister's husband'
nənəd	nəndoi
'husband's sister'	'husband's sister's husband'

ə ⟶ ø / VC -CV

20. $(X)_{n,\ sing/masc\ nom\ pl,\ inani}$ ⟷ $(X\text{ɪ}k)_{n,\ sing\ ,\ masc,\ hum,}$ *user of* X

Condition : X ends in a consonant.

pəth(masc)	pəthɪk
'path'	'traveller'
nav(fem)	navɪk
'boat'	'boatman'

21. $(X)_{n,\ sing/nom\ pl\ ani,\ masc,}$ ⟷ $(X\text{ɪ}n)_{n,\ sing,\ ani,\ fem}$

Condition: X ends in a consonant.

sunar	sunarɪn
'goldsmith'	'goldsmith's wife'
nag	nagɪn
'snake'	'female snake'

22. $(X)_{n,\ sing,\ nom.\ pl,\ masc} \longleftrightarrow (X\text{ə}k)_{n,\ sing,\ nom,\ pl,\ masc,\ hum.}$ *doer of* X

Condition: X ends in a consonant.

sʊdhar	sʊdharək
'reform'	'reformer'
lekh	lekhək
'essay'	'writer'

23. $(X)_{n,\ sing,\ fem,\ ono} \longleftrightarrow (X\text{ə}k)_{n,\ sing,\ fem,}$ *abs* X

ṭhən	ṭhənək
'jingling'	'jingling sound'
jhən	jhənək
'sound of metal striking against metal'	'clinking'

24. $(X)_{n,\ masc,\ sing} \longleftrightarrow (Xat)_{n,\ masc,\ nom,\ pl}$

Condition: X ends in a consonant.

məkan	məkanat
'house'	'houses'
səval	səvalat
'question'	'questions'

25. $(X)_{n,\ masc,\ hum,\ sing} \longleftrightarrow (Xan)_{n,\ masc,\ hum,\ nom,\ pl}$

Condition: X ends in a consonant.

malɪk	malɪkan
'master'	'masters'
kaštkar	kaštkaran
'farmer'	'farmers'

26. $(X)_{n, sing, fem} \longleftrightarrow (Xci)_{n, sing, masc,}$ *user of* X

Condition: X ends in a consonant.

top	topci
'cannon'	'cannon-keeper'
ḍholək	ḍholəkci
'drum'	'drummer'

27. $(X)_{n, sing/nom\ pl, ani, masc} \longleftrightarrow (Xni)_{n, sing, fem}$

Condition: X ends in a consonant

mor	morni
'peacock'	'female peacock'
šer	šerni
'lion'	'lioness'

28. $(X)_{n, masc, sing/nom\ pl} \longleftrightarrow (X\text{ṛa})_{n, masc, sing, nom,}$ *dimi* X

Condition: X ends in a consonant.

mʊkh	mʊkhṛa
'face'	'face' (small or dejected)
dʊkh	dʊkhṛa
'pain'	'sob-tale'

29. $(X)_{n, sing, fem} \longleftrightarrow (X\text{yã})_{n, fem, nom, pl}$

Condition: X ends in -ɪ.

šəktɪ	šəktɪyã
'power'	'powers'
tɪthɪ	tɪthɪyã
'date'	'dates'

30. $(X)_{\text{n. sing masc nom pl}} \longleftrightarrow (Xy\tilde{o})_{\text{n. obl. pl}}$

Condition: X ends in -ɪ.

kəvɪ(masc)	kəvɪyõ
'poet'	'poets'
ritɪ (fem)	rɪtɪyõ
'custom'	'customs'

31. $(X)_{\text{n. sing masc nom pl}} \longleftrightarrow (Xyo)_{\text{n. voc. pl}}$

Condition: X ends in -ɪ.

kəvɪ (masc)	kəvɪyo
'poet'	'O poets!'
ritɪ (fem)	rɪtɪyo
'custom'	'O customs!'

32. $(X)_{\text{n. sing masc nom pl}} \longleftrightarrow (X\text{ɪya})_{\text{n. sing. masc. nom.}}$ *dealer in* X

Condition: X does not end in -a.

kəbaɽ (masc)	kəbaɽɪya
'garbage'	'garbage-dealer'
ɖak (fem)	ɖakɪya
'post'	'postman'

33. $(X)_{\text{n. sing/masc nom pl}} \longleftrightarrow (X\text{ɪye})_{\text{n. masc. obl. sing/ voc nom pl}}$ *dealer(s) in* X

Condition: X does not end in -a.

aɽhət	aɽhətɪye
'commission'	'commission agent(s)'
ɖak	ɖakɪye
'post'	'postmen'

ə ⟶ o / VCC – CV

34. $(X)_{n,\ sing/masc\ nom\ pl} \longleftrightarrow (X\text{ɪyõ})_{n,\ masc,\ obl,\ pl,}$ *dealers in* X

Condition: X does not end in -a.

ḍak(fem)	ḍakɪyõ
'post'	'postmen'
kəbaṛ (masc)	kəbaṛɪyõ
'garbage'	'garbage-dealers'

35. $(X)_{n,\ sing} \longleftrightarrow (x\text{ɪyo})_{n,\ masc,\ voc,\ pl,}$ *dealers in* X

kəbaṛ (masc)	kəbaṛɪyo
'garbage'	'O garbage-dealers!'
aṛhət (fem)	aṛhtɪyo
'commission'	'O commission-agents!'

ə → ø / VCC – CV

36. $(X)_{n,\ sing} \longleftrightarrow (X\text{ɪzm})_{n,\ sing,\ abs,}$ (Xɪsm)

Condition: X is not a masculine noun ending in -a, in which case the LHS should read $(X)_{n,\ sing,\ nom.}$

brahmɪn	brahmɪnɪzm
'Brahmin'	'Brahminism'
bʊddh	bʊddhɪzm
'Buddha'	'Buddhism'

37. $(X)_{n,\ sing,\ masc} \longleftrightarrow (Xani)_{n,\ sing,\ fem}$

mehtər	mehtrani
'sweeper'	'sweeperess'
seṭh	seṭhani
'merchant'	'merchant's wife'

ə → ø / VCC – CV

38. $(X)_{\text{n. masc. sing}} \longleftrightarrow (Xana)_{\text{n. masc. sing. nom.}}$ *related to* X

Condition: X ends in a consonant.

ghər	ghərana
'house'	'lineage'
dost	dostana
'friend'	'friendship'

39. $(X)_{\text{n. sing/masc nom pl}} \longleftrightarrow (Xkar)_{\text{n. sing. masc.}}$ *creator of* X

Condition: A masculine X does not end in -a.

cɪtr (masc)	cɪtrkar
'painting'	'painter'
kəla (fem)	kəlakar
'art'	'artist'

40. $(X)_{\text{n. sing. ono}} \longleftrightarrow (Xkar)_{\text{n. sing.}}$ *abs* X

pʊc	pʊckar (fem)
'ono. sound showing love'	'an affectionate call'
haha	hahakar (masc)
'ono. sound showing sorrow'	'lamentation'

41. $(X)_{\text{n. sing/masc nom pl}} \longleftrightarrow (Xgər)_{\text{n. sing. masc.}}$ *doer of* X

Condition: A masculine X does not end in -a.

jadu (masc)	jadugər
'magic'	'magician'
bazi (fem)	bazigər
'game'	'juggler'

42. $(X)_{\text{n, sing/masc nom pl}} \longleftrightarrow (X\text{dan})_{\text{n, sing, masc,}}$ *container for* X

Condition: A masculine X does not end in -a.

phul (masc)	phuldan
'flower'	'flower-vase'
qələm (fem)	qələmdan
'pen'	'pen-stand'

43. $(X)_{\text{n, sing/masc nom pl}} \longleftrightarrow (X\text{dar})_{\text{n, sing, masc,}}$ *having* X

Condition: A masculine X does not end in -a except in the case of its nominative singular form.

mal (masc)	maldar
'wealth'	'wealthy man'
zəmĩ (fem)	zəmĩdar
'land'	'landlord'

44. $(X)_{\text{n, sing/nom pl masc}} \longleftrightarrow (X\text{pən})_{\text{n, sing, masc,}}$ *state of being* X

Condition: X does not end in -a.

pagəl	pagəlpən
'mad'	'madness'
šɪšu	šɪšupən
'child'	'childhood'

45. $(X)_{\text{n, sing, fem}} \longleftrightarrow (X\text{baz})_{\text{n, sing, masc,}}$ *skilled user of* X

pətəŋ	pətəŋbaz
'kite'	'kite flyer'
cal	calbaz
'trick'	'trickster'

46. $(X)_{n,\ sing} \longleftrightarrow (Xsaz)_{n,\ sing,\ masc,}$ *maker of* X

Condition: A masculine X does not end in -a.

ghəṛi (fem)	ghəṛisaz
'watch'	'watch-maker'
jal (masc)	jalsaz
'net'	'net-maker'

47. $(X)_{n,\ sing} \longleftrightarrow (Xxor)_{n,\ sing,\ masc,}$ *indulging in* X

ghus (fem)	ghusxor
'bribe'	'taker of bribes'
sud (masc)	sudxor
'interest'	'usurer'

48. $(X)_{n,\ sing,\ abs} \longleftrightarrow (Xvan)_{n,\ sing,\ masc,}$ *posessor of* X

dhən (masc)	dhənvan
'money'	'rich person'
vɪdya (fem)	vɪdyavan
'knowledge'	'scholar'

49. $(X)_{n,\ sing} \longleftrightarrow (X\text{ɪyət})_{n,\ sing,fem,}$ *abs* X

Condition: X ends in a consonant.

ɪnsan (masc)	ɪnsanɪyət
'man'	'humanness'
kəbz (fem)	kəbzɪyət
'constipation'	'state of constipation'

50. $(X)_{n,\ sing} \longleftrightarrow (X\text{aləy})_{n,\ sing,\ masc,}$ *place of* X

pustək (fem)	pustakaləy
'book'	'library'
səcɪv (masc)	səcɪvaləy
'secretary'	'secretariat'
mədɪra (fem)	mədɪraləy
'liquor'	'pub'

1. $ə \rightarrow ø / C - CV$
2. $a \rightarrow ø / VC - aC$

51. $(X)_{n,\ sing,\ masc} \longleftrightarrow (X\ gɪrɪ)_{n,\ sing,\ fem,}$ *what* X *does*

neta (hon)	netagɪrɪ
'leader'	'leadership'
kʊlɪ	kʊligɪrɪ
'porter'	'portering'

52. $(X)_{n,\ sing} \longleftrightarrow (Xn)_{n,\ inani,\ nom,\ sing,\ masc,}$ *document pertaining to* X

hʊkm (masc)	hʊkmnama
'order'	'document containing the order'
mʊkhtar	mʊkhtarnama
'attorney'	'power of attorney'

53. $(X)_{n,\ sing} \longleftrightarrow (Xvala)_{n,\ nom\ sing\ masc,}$ *dealing in* X

dudh (masc)	dudhvala
'milk'	'milkman'
kʊrsi (fem)	kʊrsivala
'chair'	'one who sells or repairs chairs'

(C) *Suffixation with morphophonemic changes* (WFSs 54-61)

54. $(P\ \underset{\substack{-\text{high}\\+\text{long}}}{V}\ Ca)_{n,masc,nom,sing} \longleftrightarrow (P\ \underset{\substack{+\text{high}\\-\text{long}}}{V}\ Cr)_{n,masc,sing,}$ *one who deals in* X

sona	sʊnar
'gold'	'goldsmith'
loha	lʊhar
'iron'	'ironsmith'

55. (PaCV)$_{\text{n, nom, sing}}$ ⟷ (PəCæt)$_{\text{n, masc, sing,}}$ *practising* X

ɖaka	ɖəkæt
'robbery'	'robber'
laʈhi	ləʈhæt
'stick'	'stick-wielding'

56. (PV)$_{\text{n, masc}}$ ⟷ (Pɪn)$_{\text{n, sing, fem}}$

səpera	səperɪn
'snake-charmer'	'snake-charmer's wife'
teli	telɪn
'oil-dealer'	'female oil-dealer/oil-dealer's wife'

57. $\left(\text{P } \underset{\begin{smallmatrix}\text{- high}\\ \text{+ long}\end{smallmatrix}}{\text{V}} \text{ Q}\right)_{\text{n, masc, sing}}$ ⟷ $\left(\text{P } \underset{\begin{smallmatrix}\text{+ high}\\ \text{- long}\end{smallmatrix}}{\text{V}} \text{ Qai}\right)_{\text{n, fem, sing,}}$ *abs* X

ʈhakʊr	ʈhəkurai
'a caste-name'	'arrongance of Thakurs'
kam	kəmai
'work'	'earnings'

58. (PVQ)$_{\text{n, sing}}$ ⟷ (PVQari)$_{\text{n, sing, masc}}$ *related to* X

bhikh	bhɪkhari
'alms'	'beggar'

59. (PVCQ)$_{\text{n, nom, sing}}$ ⟷ (PVCɪya)$_{\text{n, nom, sing}}$ *dimi of* X

khaʈ	khəʈɪya
'bed'	'small bed'
cuha	cʊhɪya
'rat'	'small rat/female rat'

60. $(\underset{\substack{-\text{high}\\+\text{long}}}{\text{P V}}\ \text{CQ})_{\text{n, sing, nom}} \longleftrightarrow (\underset{\substack{+\text{high}\\-\text{long}}}{\text{P V}}\ \text{Cɪya})_{\text{n,nom, sing}}$ *dimi of* X

beṭa	bɪṭɪya
'son'	'daughter (affectionate)'
coṭi	cʊṭɪya
'pony tail'	'small pony tail'

61. $(\text{PaQ})_{\text{n, sing}} \longleftrightarrow (\text{PəQola})_{\text{n, sing, nom,}}$ *dimi of* X

khaṭ	khəṭola
'bed'	'small bed'
sã̄p	sə̃pola
'snake'	'small snake'

(d) *Prefixation* (WFSs 62-86)

62. $(\text{X})_{\text{n, sing, abs}} \longleftrightarrow (\text{əX})_{\text{n, sing, abs}}$ *opposite of* X

səty(masc)	əsəty
'truth'	'untruth'
səhmətɪ (fem)	əsəhmətɪ
'agreement'	'disagreement'

63. $(\text{X})_{\text{n, sing, abs}} \longleftrightarrow (\text{əvX})_{\text{n, sing, abs,}}$ *specific* X

ləmb (masc)	əvləmb
'perpendicular'	'support'
dharṇa (fem)	əvdharṇa
'belief'	'specific belief'

64. $(\text{X})_{\text{n, sing}} \longleftrightarrow (\text{ʊpX})_{\text{n, sing,}}$ *junior to or smaller than* X

kʊlpətɪ	ʊpkʊlpətɪ
'chancellor'	'vice-chancellor'
nəgər	ʊpnəgər
'town'	'small town'

65. $(X)_{n,\ sing,\ abs} \longleftrightarrow (\text{ʊ}dX)_{n,\ sing,\ abs,}$ *related to* X

bhavna (fem)	ʊdbhavna
'emotion'	'imagination'
ghoš (masc)	ʊdghoš
'sound'	'proclamation'

66. $(X)_{n,\ sing} \longleftrightarrow (k\text{ʊ}X)_{n,\ sing,}$ *bad* X

patr (masc)	kʊpatr
'deserving person'	'underserving person'
cal (fem)	kʊcal
'move'	'bad move'

67. $(X)_{n,\ sing,\ abs} \longleftrightarrow (beX)_{n,\ sing,\ abs,}$ X *lessness*

vəfai	bevəfai
'faithfulness'	'faithlessness'
rozgari	berozgari
'employment'	'unemployment'

68. $(X)_{n,\ sing,\ abs,} \longleftrightarrow (beX)_{n,\ sing,}$ *person without* X

ɪman (masc)	beɪman
'honesty'	'dishonest'
vəfa (fem)	bevəfa
'sincerity'	'insincere'

69. $(X)_{n,\ sing} \longleftrightarrow (naX)_{n,\ sing,}$ *not* X

balɪg (masc)	nabalɪg
'major'	'minor'
ɪnsaf	naɪnsaf
'justice'	'injustice'

70. $(X)_{n,\ sing} \longleftrightarrow (səX)_{n,\ sing,}$ *good* X

put	səput
'son'	'good son'
jən	səjən
'person'	'good person'

71. (X)$_{\text{n. sing}}$ ⟷ (sʊX)$_{\text{n. sing.}}$ *good* X

pʊtr (masc)	sʊpʊtr
'son'	'good son'
gəndh (fem)	sʊgəndh
'smell'	'pleasant smell'

72. (X)$_{\text{n. sing}}$ ⟷ (vɪX)$_{\text{n. sing.}}$ *opposite of* X

krey (masc)	vɪkrey
'purchase'	'sale'
krɪtɪ (fem)	vɪkrɪtɪ
'creation'	'deformed creation'

73. (X)$_{\text{n. sing}}$ ⟷ (vɪX)$_{\text{n. sing.}}$ *intensified* X

nəmrəta (fem)	vɪnəmrəta
'modesty'	'extreme modesty'
droh (mas)	vɪdroh
'hostility'	'rebellion'

74. (X)$_{\text{n. sing. masc}}$ ⟷ (ədhɪX)$_{\text{n. sing. masc.}}$ *special* X

nayək	ədhɪnayək
'leader'	'supreme leader'
niyəm	ədhiniyəm
'rule'	'act'

75. (X)$_{\text{n. sing}}$ ⟷ (əbhiX)$_{\text{n. sing.}}$ *excess of* X

rəkša (fem)	əbhɪrəkša
'protection'	'special protection'
man (masc)	əbhɪman
'respect'	'arrogance'

76. (X)$_{\text{n. sing}}$ ⟷ (ənʊX)$_{\text{n. sing.}}$ *following or involving* X

mətɪ (fem)	ənʊməti
'view'	'approval'
vad (masc)	ənʊvad
'discussion'	'translation'

77. $(X)_{n,\ sing} \longleftrightarrow (pəṛX)_{n,\ sing,}$ *great/other* X

baba (masc)	pəṛbaba
'grandfather'	'great grandfather'
nani (fem)	pəṛnani
'grandmother (maternal)'	'great grandmother'

78. $(X)_{n,\ sing} \longleftrightarrow (prəX)_{n,\ sing,}$ *intensified* X

kop (masc)	prəkop
'anger'	'fury'
krɪya	prəkrɪya
'action'	'activity'

79. $(X)_{n,\ sing} \longleftrightarrow (dʊrX)_{n,\ sing,}$ *bad* X

bhagy (masc)	dʊrbhagy
'fate'	'bad luck'
gəndh (fem)	dʊrgəndh
'smell'	'bad smell'

80. $(X)_{n,\ sing} \longleftrightarrow (sərX)_{n,\ sing,}$ *head of* X

taj (masc)	sərtaj
'crown'	'supreme king'
həd (fem)	sərhəd
'limit'	'border' (territorial)

81. $(X)_{n,\ sing,\ masc} \longleftrightarrow (səhX)_{n,\ sing,\ masc,}$ co-X

yatri	səhyatri
'traveller'	'co-traveller'
paṭhi	səhpaṭhi
'student'	'class fellow'

82. $(X)_{n,\ sing,\ nom} \longleftrightarrow (həmX)_{n,\ sing\ masc}$ *person with the same* X *as the speaker*

vətən	həmvətən
'country'	'fellow countryman'

səfər	həmsəfər
'journey'	'co-traveller'

83. $(X)_{n, sing, masc} \longleftrightarrow (svəX)_{n, sing, masc}$ *own* X

deš	swədeš
'country'	'own country'
dhərm	swədhərm
'religion'	'own religion'

84. $(X)_{n, sing, abs, masc} \longleftrightarrow (pərɪX)_{n, sing, abs, masc}$ *intensified* X

tyag	pərɪtyag
'sacrifice'	'renunciation'
'purɳ'	'pərɪpurɳ
'complete'	'absolutely complete'

85. $(X)_{n, sing} \longleftrightarrow (prətɪX)_{n, sing,}$ *per or every* X

mah	prətɪmah
'month'	'per or every month'
vərš	prətɪvərš
'year'	'per or every year'

86. $(X)_{n, sing} \longleftrightarrow (prətɪX)_{n, sing,}$ *counter* X

ghat (masc)	prətɪghat
'attack'	'counter-attack'
hɪnsa (fem)	prətɪhinsa
'violence'	'counter-violence'

(e) *Substitution* (WFSs 87-99)

87. $(Pa)_{n, nom, sing, masc} \longleftrightarrow (Pi)_{n, sing, fem}$

ləɽka	ləɽki
'boy'	'girl'

bəkra	bəkri
'goat'	'she-goat'

88. $(\mathrm{Pa})_{\text{n. nom. sing. masc}} \longleftrightarrow (\mathrm{Pe})_{\text{n. masc. obl sing voc sing nom pl}}$

ghoɽa	ghoɽe
'horse'	'horses'
məkbəra	məkbəre
'tomb'	'tombs'

89. $(\mathrm{Pa})_{\text{n. masc. nom. sing}} \longleftrightarrow (\mathrm{Po})_{\text{n. masc. voc. pl}}$

kəmra	kəmro
'room'	'O rooms!'
ləɽka	ləɽko
'boy'	'O boys!'

90. $(\mathrm{Pa})_{\text{n. masc. nom. sing}} \longleftrightarrow (\mathrm{P\tilde{o}})_{\text{n. masc. obl. pl}}$

dərvaza	dərvazõ
'door'	'doors'
ləɽka	ləɽkõ
'boy'	'boys'

91. $(\mathrm{Pa})_{\text{n. sing. fem}} \longleftrightarrow (\mathrm{P\partial k})_{\text{n. sing. masc}}$ *doer of* X

šikša	šikšək
'education'	'educator'
parikša	pərikšək
'examination'	'examiner'

92. $(\mathrm{Pa})_{\text{n. masc. sing. nom}} \longleftrightarrow (\mathrm{Pu})_{\text{n. masc. sing.}}$ *endeared* X

šera	šeru
'Shera' (name)	'Sheru'
kəlla	kəllu
'Kalla' (name)	'Kallu'

93. (Pa)$_{\text{n. sing. fem}}$ ⟷ (Pe)$_{\text{n. sing fem. voc}}$

sita	site
'Sita'	'O Sita!'
prɪya	prɪye
'beloved'	'O beloved!'

94. (Pi)$_{\text{n. sing. fem}}$ ⟷ (Pa)$_{\text{n. sing. masc.}}$ *big* X

gəṭhṛi	ghəṭhṛa
'bundle'	'big bundle'
cɪṭṭhi	cɪṭṭha
'letter'	'long letter'

95. (Pi)$_{\text{n. sing fem}}$ ⟷ (Pɪyã)$_{\text{n. fem. pl. nom}}$

ləṛki	ləṛkɪyã
'girl'	'girls'
ghəṛi	ghəṛɪyã
'watch'	'watches'

96. (Pi)$_{\text{n. fem. sing}}$ ⟷ (Pɪyõ)$_{\text{n. fem. pl. obl}}$

dəri	dərɪyõ
'mat'	'mats'
kʊrsi	kʊrsɪyõ
'chair'	'chairs'

97. (Pi)$_{\text{n. fem. sing}}$ ⟷ (Pɪyo)$_{\text{n. fem. pl. voc}}$

kʊrsi	kʊrsɪyo
'chair'	'O chairs!'
ləṛki	ləṛkɪyo
'girl'	'O girls!'

98. (Pɔk)$_{\text{n. sing. masc}}$ ⟷ (Pɪka)$_{\text{n. sing. nom. fem}}$

balɔk	balɪka
'boy'	'small girl'

ədhyapək	ədhyapıka
'teacher'	'teacheress'

99. $(Xna)_{n, sing, fem} \longleftrightarrow (Xək)_{n, sing, masc,}$ *doer of* X

sadhna	sadhək
'meditation'	'meditator'
bhavna	bhavək
'sentiment'	'care-taker'

8.2 *Verbs and Nouns* (B)

(a) *Identity* (WFSs 100-101)

100. $(X)_{v, imper, nh} \longleftrightarrow (X)_{n, sing}$

mar	mar (fem)
'beat'	'beating'
khel	khel (masc)
'play'	'game'

101. $(X)_{v, imper} \longleftrightarrow (X)_{n, voc, pl}$

Condition: X ends in -o.

naco	naco (masc)
'dance'	'O dances!'
pʊkaro	pʊkaro (fem)
'call'	'O calls!'

(b) *Suffixation* (WFSs 102 - 114)

102. $(X)_{v, imper, nh} \longleftrightarrow (Xe)_{n, nom, fem, pl}$

mar	marẽ
'beat'	'beatings'
pʊkar	pʊkarẽ
'call'	'calls'

103. $(X)_{v.\ imper.\ nh} \longleftrightarrow (Xo)_{n.\ voc.\ pl}$

nac	naco (masc)
'dance	'O dances!'
mar	maro (fem)
'beat'	'O beatings!'

104. $(X)_{v.\ imper.\ nh} \longleftrightarrow (X\tilde{o})_{n.\ obl.\ pl}$

pʊkar	pʊkarõ (fem)
'call'	'calls'
nac	nacõ (masc)
'dance'	'dances'

105. $(X)_{v.\ imper.\ nh} \longleftrightarrow (X\text{ə}k)_{n.\ sing}$

sadh	sadhək (masc)
'accomplish'	'accomplisher'
bæʈh	bæʈhək (fem)
'sit'	'living room'

106. $(X)_{v.\ imper.\ nh} \longleftrightarrow (X\text{ə}n)_{n.\ sing}$

jəl	jələn (fem)
'be jealous'	'jealousy'
mɪl	mɪlən (masc)
'meet'	'meeting'

107. $(X)_{v.\ imper.\ nh} \longleftrightarrow (Xai)_{n.\ fem.\ sing}$

ləɽ	ləɽai
'fight'	'fight'
lɪkh	lɪkhai
'write'	'writing'

108. $(X)_{v.\ imper.\ nh} \longleftrightarrow (Xan)_{n.\ sing.\ abs}$

thək	thəkan (fem)
'tire'	'fatigue'
ləg	ləgan (masc)
'work'	'agricultural revenue'

109. $(X)_{v.\ imper.\ nh} \longleftrightarrow (Xav)_{n.\ masc.\ sing}$

cɪn	cɪnav
'elect'	'election'
bəh	bəhav
'flow'	'flow'

110. $(X)_{v.\ imper.\ nh} \longleftrightarrow (Xni)_{n.\ fem.\ sing}$

kəh	kəhni
'say'	'saying'
kər	kərni
'do'	'doing'

111. $(X)_{v.\ imper.\ nh} \longleftrightarrow (Xna)_{n.\ nom.\ sing.\ masc}$

ro	rona
'cry'	'crying'
kha	khana
'eat'	'food'

112 $(X)_{v.\ imper.nh} \longleftrightarrow (Xva)_{n.\ nom.\ masc.\ sing}$

pəchta	pəchtava
'repent'	'repentence'
dɪkha	dɪkhava
'show'	'ostentation'

113. $(X)_{v.\ imper.\ nh} \longleftrightarrow (Xvəʈ)_{n.\ sing.\ fem.\ abs}$

dɪkha	dikhavəʈ
'show'	'ostentation'
bəna	bənavəʈ
'make'	'affectation'

114. $(X)_{v.\ imper.\ nh} \longleftrightarrow (Xhəʈ)_{n.\ sing.\ fem.\ ono}$

bhɪnbhɪna	bhɪnbhɪnahəʈ
'buzz'	'buzzing'

gɪɽgɪɽa	gɪɽgɪɽahəʈ
'beg'	'entreaty'

(c) *Deletion* (WFS 115)

115. $(Xa)_{v.imper.nh} \longleftrightarrow (X)_{n.\ sing}$

ləhəra	ləhər (fem)
'swing'	'wave'
dʊkha	dʊkh (masc)
'hurt'	'pain'

(d) *Deletion with morphophonemic change* (WFSs 116-117)

116. $(CəCa)_{v.\ imper.\ nh} \longleftrightarrow (CaC)_{n.\ sing}$

kəma	kam (masc)
'earn'	'work'
bəta	bat (fem)
'tell'	'talk'

117. $(PəQɪya)_{v.\ imper.\ nh} \longleftrightarrow (PaQ)_{n.\ sing}$

bətɪya	bat (fem)
'talk'	'talk'
həthɪya	hath (masc)
'appropriate'	'hand'

8.3 *Nouns and Adjectives* (C)

(a) *Identity* (WFSs 118-125)

118. $(Xi)_{n.\ masc.\ sing} \longleftrightarrow (Xi)_{adj}$

əpradhi	əpradhi
'a criminal'	'criminal'
doši	doši
'a guilty person'	'guilty'

119. $(Xbaz)_{n, masc, sing} \longleftrightarrow (Xbaz)_{adj}$

calbaz	calbaz
'trickster'	'crafty'
pətəŋbaz	pətəŋbaz
'kite-flyer'	'kite-flying'

120. $(Xvər)_{n, masc, sing} \longleftrightarrow (Xvər)_{adj}$

takətvər	takətvər
'strong man'	'strong'
tajvər	tajvər
'king'	'crowned'

121. $(Xvar)_{n, masc, sing} \longleftrightarrow (Xvar)_{adj}$

kəsurvar	kəsurvar
'guilty man'	'guilty'
ʊmmedvar	ʊmmedvar
'contestant'	'hopeful' (in election)

122. $(Xvan)_{n, masc, sing} \longleftrightarrow (Xvan)_{adj}$

bəlvan	bəlvan
'strong man'	'strong'
dhənvan	dhənvan
'wealthy man'	'wealthy'

123. $(Xmənd)_{n, masc, sing} \longleftrightarrow (Xmənd)_{adj}$

dɔlətmənd	dɔlətmənd
'rich man'	'rich'
zərurətmənd	zərurətmənd
'needy man'	'needy'

124. $(Xəsvi)_{n, masc, sing} \longleftrightarrow (Xəsvi)_{adj}$

tejəsvi	tejəsvi
'enlightened'	'enlightened'

yəšəsvi	yəšəsvi
'man of honour'	'honourable'

125. $(\text{Xəndaz})_{\text{n. masc. sing}} \longleftrightarrow (\text{Xəndaz})_{\text{adj}}$

tirəndaz	tirəndaz
'archer'	'knowing archery'
dəstəndaz	dəstəndaz
'meddler'	'meddling'

(b) *Suffixation* (WFSs 126-154)

126. $(\text{X})_{\text{n. sing}} \longleftrightarrow (\text{Xi})_{\text{adj}}$

Condition: X ends in a consonant.

kɪtab (fem)	kɪtabi
'book'	'bookish'
gʊlab	gʊlabi
'rose'	'rosy'

127. $(\text{X})_{\text{n. sing}} \longleftrightarrow (\text{Xa})_{\text{adj}}$

Condition: X ends in a consonant.

mæl (fem)	mæla
'dirt'	'dirty'
pyar (masc)	pyara
'love'	'lovely'

128. $(\text{X})_{\text{n. sing}} \longleftrightarrow (\text{Xɪt})_{\text{adj}}$

kələŋk (masc)	kələŋkɪt
'blemish'	'blemished'
jəɽ	jəɽɪt
'root'	'immobilised'

129. $(\text{X})_{\text{n. masc. sing}} \longleftrightarrow (\text{Xin})_{\text{adj}}$

kʊl	kʊlin
'lineage'	'belonging to a noble family'

rəŋ	rəŋin
'colour'	'colourful'

130. $(X)_{n, sing} \longleftrightarrow (X\text{ɪl})_{adj}$

bojh (masc)	bojhɪl
'burden'	'burdensome'
phen (fem)	phenɪl
'foam'	'foamy'

131. $(X)_{n, sing} \longleftrightarrow (X\text{dã})_{adj}$

kədr (fem)	kədrdã
'respect'	'one who respects'
kanun(masc)	kanundã
'law'	'knowing law'

132. $(X)_{n, fem, sing} \longleftrightarrow (X\text{lʊ})_{adj}$

dəya	dəyalʊ
'kindness'	'kind'
krɪpa	krɪpalʊ
'kindness'	'kind'

133. $(X)_{n, masc, sing} \longleftrightarrow (X\text{ɪya})_{adj}$

kesər	kesərɪya
'saffron'	'saffron-coloured'
dudh	dudhɪya
'milk'	'milky'

134. $(X)_{n, masc, sing} \longleftrightarrow (X\text{ida})_{adj}$

rə̃j	rə̃jida
'suffering'	'suffering'
pec	pecida
'complication'	'complicated'

135. $(X)_{n, sing} \longleftrightarrow (X\text{ila})_{adj}$

xərc (masc)	xərcila
'expenditure'	'extravagant'

cəmək (fem)	cəmkila
'shine'	'shining'
ə → o / VC – CV	

136. $(X)_{n.\ sing} \longleftrightarrow (Xani)_{adj}$

bərf (fem)	bərfani
'ice/snow'	'icy/snowy'
jɪsm	jɪsmani
'body'	'bodily'

137. $(X)_{n.\ masc.\ sing} \longleftrightarrow (Xana)_{adj}$

mərd	mərdana
'man'	'manly'
šayər	šayərana
'poet'	'poetic'

138. $(X)_{n.\ sing} \longleftrightarrow (Xgar)_{adj}$

mədəd (fem)	mədədgar
'help'	'helping'
gʊnah (masc)	gʊnahgar
'sin'	'sinning'

139. $(X)_{n.\ sing} \longleftrightarrow (Xdar)_{adj}$

phəl (masc)	phəldar
'fruit/reward'	'full of fruit/profitable'
šan (fem)	šandar
'splendour'	'splenderous'

140. $(X)_{n.\ sing} \longleftrightarrow (Xbaz)_{adj}$

pətəŋ (fem)	pətəŋbaz
'kite'	'having ability to fly kites'
bəmb (masc)	bəmbaz
'bomb'	'having expertise in handling bombs'

141. $(X)_{n.\ sing} \longleftrightarrow (Xnak)_{adj}$

dərd (masc)	dərdnak
'pain'	'painful'
šərm (fem)	šərmnak
'shame'	'shameful'

142. $(X)_{n.\ masc.\ sing} \longleftrightarrow (Xniy)_{adj}$

man	manniy
'honour'	'honourable'
adər	aderniy
'respect'	'respectable'

143. $(X)_{n.\ sing} \longleftrightarrow (Xməy)_{adj}$

bhav (masc)	bhavməy
'sentiment'	'sentimental'
maya	mayaməy
'illusion'	'illusory'

144. $(X)_{n.\ sing} \longleftrightarrow (Xxez)_{adj}$

sənsəni (fem)	sənsənixez
'sensation'	'sensational'
zər (masc)	zərxez
'wealth'	'fertile'

145. $(X)_{n.\ masc.\ sing} \longleftrightarrow (Xvan)_{adj}$

bəl	bəlvan
'power'	'powerful'
dhən	dhənvan
'wealth'	'wealthy'

146. $(X)_{\text{n. nom. sing}} \longleftrightarrow (Xvər)_{\text{adj}}$

nam (masc)	namvər
'name'	'famous'
takət (fem)	takətvər
'strength'	'strong'

147. $(X)_{\text{n. sing}} \longleftrightarrow (Xvar)_{\text{adj}}$

kəsur (masc)	kəsurvar
'mistake'	'guilty'
ʊmmed (fem)	ʊmmedvar
'hope'	'hopeful'

148. $(X)_{\text{n. sing}} \longleftrightarrow (\bar{X}sar)_{\text{adj}}$

xak (fem)	xaksar
'ashes'	'personal address form' (insignificant self)
milən (masc)	milənsar
'meeting'	'sociable'

149. $(X)_{\text{n. masc. sing}} \longleftrightarrow (Xəsvi)_{\text{adj}}$

tej	tejəsvi
'glow'	'having glow'
yəš	yəšəsvi
'honour'	'well-known'

150. $(X)_{\text{n. sing}} \longleftrightarrow (Xnʊma)_{\text{adj}}$

kəṭori (fem)	kəṭorinʊma
'small-bowl'	'bowl-like'
gʊmbəd	gʊmbədnʊma
'dome'	'dome-like'

151. $(X)_{n,\ sing} \longleftrightarrow (Xmənd)_{adj}$

hʊnər (masc)	hʊnərmənd
'skill'	'skillful'
gərz (fem)	gərzmənd
'need'	'needy'

152. $(X)_{n,\ sing} \longleftrightarrow (Xšʊda)_{adj}$

šadi (fem)	šadišʊda
'marriage'	'married'
gəm (masc)	gəmšʊda
'pain'	'suffering'

153. $(X)_{n,\ sing} \longleftrightarrow (Xvənt)_{adj}$

kəla (fem)	kəlavənt
'art'	'artistic'
dhən (masc)	dhənvənt
'money'	'moneyed'

154. $(X)_{n,\ masc,\ sing} \longleftrightarrow (Xəndaz)_{adj}$

tir	tirəndaz
'arrow'	'having expertise in archery'
dəst	dəstəndaz
'hand'	'meddling'

(c) *Suffixation with morphophonemic change* (WFSs 155-157)

155. $((C)əP)_{n,\ masc,\ sing} \longleftrightarrow ((C)aPɪk)_{adj}$

ərth	arthɪk
'money'	'monetary'
pəkš	pakšɪk
'fortnight'	'fortnightly'

156. $((P)ɪQ)_{n,\ masc,\ sing} \longleftrightarrow ((P)aɪQɪk)_{adj}$

ɪtɪhas	aɪtɪhasɪk
'history'	'historical'
vɪdhan	vaɪdhanɪk
'legislation'	'constitutional'

(d) *Prefixation* (WFSs 157 - 163)

157. $(CVC)_{n,\ nom,\ sing} \longleftrightarrow (C\check{V}Cæl)_{adj}$

dudh	dʊdhæl
'milk'	'milky'
dag	dəgæl
'mark'	'spotted'

158. $(X)_{n,\ sing} \longleftrightarrow (əX)_{adj,}$ *opposite of* X

kal	əkal
'time'	'untimely'
drɪšy	ədrɪšy
'sight'	'invisible'

159. $(X)_{n,\ nom,\ masc,\ sing} \longleftrightarrow (nɪX)_{adj,}$ *without* X

ḍər	nɪḍər
'fear'	'without fear'
bəl	nɪbəl
'strength'	'without strength'

160. $(X)_{n,\ nom,\ sing} \longleftrightarrow (laX)_{adj,\ neg}$ X*less*

varɪs (masc)	lavarɪs
'heir'	'heirless'
pərvah (fem)	lapərvah
'care'	'careless'

161. $(X)_{n,\ nom,\ sing} \longleftrightarrow (həmX)_{adj}$

dərd (masc)	həmdərd
'pain'	'sympathetic'
rah (fem)	həmrah
'path'	'co-traveller'

162. $(X)_{n, nom, masc, sing} \longleftrightarrow (nɪrX)_{adj, neg}$ X*less*

adhar	nɪradhar
'base'	'baseless'
ahar	nɪrahar
'food'	'without food'

163. $(X)_{n, masc, sing} \longleftrightarrow (nɪšX)_{adj, neg}$ X *less*

pəkš	nɪšpəkš
'side'	'unbiased'
phəl	nɪšphəl
'result'	'ineffective'

(e) *Substitution* (WFSs 164-165).

164. $(Pa)_{n, masc, sing} \longleftrightarrow (Pedar)_{adj}$

məza	məzedar
'fun'	'interesting'
pəṭakha	pəṭakhedar
'cracker'	'explosive'

165. $(Pna)_{n, nom, fem, sing} \longleftrightarrow (Pniy)_{adj}$

sərahna	sərahniy
'praise'	'praiseworthy'
'sadhna'	'sadhniy'
practice	worth attaining

(f) *Substitution with morphophonemic change* (WFSs 166-167)

166 $((P)ɪQa)_{n, nom, fem, sing} \longleftrightarrow ((P)aɪQɪk)_{adj}$

šɪkša	šaɪkšɪk
'education'	'educational'
ɪccha	aɪcchɪk
'desire'	'desired'

167. $(\text{CaCa})_{\text{n. masc. sing}} \longleftrightarrow (\text{CəCera})_{\text{adj}}$

mama	məmera
'maternal uncle'	'related through *mama*'
caca	cəcera
'paternal uncle'	'related through *caca*'

8.4 *Nouns and Adverbs* (D)

(a) *Suffixation* (WFSs 168-170)

168. $(\text{X})_{\text{n. nom. sing}} \longleftrightarrow (\text{Xən})_{\text{adv}}$

kudrət (fem)	kudrətən
'nature'	'by itself'
əndaz (masc)	əndazən
'guess'	'approximately'

169. $(\text{X})_{\text{n. sing. ono}} \longleftrightarrow (\text{Xak})_{\text{adv}}$

pəṭ	pəṭak
'ono sound'	'a loud sound'
səṭ	səṭak
'ono sound'	'sound of a whip–strike'

170. $(\text{X})_{\text{n. nom. sing}} \longleftrightarrow (\text{Xvar})_{\text{adv. frequency}}$

mah	mahvar
'month'	'monthly'
tərtib	tərtibvar
'order'	'in proper sequence'

(b) *Prefixation* (WFSs 171-174)

171. $(\text{X})_{\text{n. nom. sing}} \longleftrightarrow (\text{bəX})_{\text{adv}}$

dəstur (masc)	bədəstur
'custom'	'according to custom'
xubi (fem)	bəxubi
'speciality'	'excellently'

172. $(X)_{n.\ nom.\ sing} \longleftrightarrow (baX)_{adv}$

vəjud (masc)	bavəjud
'existence'	'in spite of'
abru (fem)	baabru
'honour'	'with honour'

173. $(X)_{n.\ nom.\ masc.\ sing} \longleftrightarrow (beX)_{adv}$

šəq	bešəq
'doubt'	'undoubtedly'
vəqt	bevəqt
'time'	'untimely'

174. $(X)_{n.\ nom.\ sing} \longleftrightarrow (s\partial X)_{adv}$ *with* X

pərivar (masc)	səpərivar
'family'	'with family'
deh (fem)	sədeh
'body'	'with body'

(c) *Substitution* (WFS 175)

175. $(Xa)_{n.\ nom.\ masc\ sing} \longleftrightarrow (Xe)_{adv}$

səvera	səvere
'morning'	'in the morning'
samna	samne
'confrontation'	'in front of'

8.5 *Verbs and Verbs* (E)

(In the description that follows, the symbol 'v' for verb stands for '2nd person, singular, non-honorific imperative'.)

(a) *Identity* (WFSs 176-197)

176. $(X)_{v.\ masc} \longleftrightarrow (X)_{v.\ fem}$

cəl	cəl
'you (masc) walk'	'you (fem) walk'

lɪkh	lɪkh
'you (masc) write'	'you (fem) write'

177. $(X)_v \longleftrightarrow (X)_{v,\ Ist\ caus}$

Condition : X ends in -a.

ghəbra	ghəbra
'be nervous'	'cause somebody to be nervous'
šərma	šərma
'feel shy'	'cause somebody to be shy'

178. $(X)_v \longleftrightarrow (X)_{v,\ IInd\ caus}$

Condition: X ends in *-a*.

jəgməga	jəgməga
'glitter'	'cause somebody to cause something to glitter'
ghəbra	ghəbra
'be nervous'	'cause somebody to cause' somebody to be nervous'

179. $(Xi)_{v,\ pert,\ fem,\ sing,\ I} \longleftrightarrow (Xi)_{v,\ perf,\ fem,\ sing\ IInh/\ III}$

cəli	cəli
'I (fem) walked'	'you (fem)/she walked'
roi	roi
'I (fem) cried'	'you (fem)/she cried'

180. $(X\tilde{i})_{v,\ perf,\ fem,\ pl,\ I} \longleftrightarrow (X\tilde{i})_{v,\ perf,\ fem,\ pl,\ II/III}$

cəlĩ	cəlĩ
'we (fem) walked'	'you (fem, pl)/they walked'
bhagĩ	bhagĩ
'we(fem) ran'	'you (fem, pl)/they ran'

181. $(Xe)_{v,\ perf,\ masc,\ pl,\ I} \longleftrightarrow (Xe)_{v,\ perf,\ masc\ pl\ II/\ III}$

bhage	bhage
'we ran'	'you(pl)/they ran'
cəle	cəle
'we walked'	'you (pl)/they walked'

182. $(X\tilde{e})_{v,\ opt,\ sing,\ II,\ nh} \longleftrightarrow (X\tilde{e})_{v,\ opt,\ sing,\ III}$

cəlẽ	cəlẽ
'(if you wish to) come'	'(if he wishes to) come'
kholẽ	kholẽ
'(if you) open'	'(if he) opens'

183. $(Xe)_{v,\ perf,\ masc,\ pl} \longleftrightarrow (Xe)_{v,\ sing,\ II.nh/III\ opt}$

bhage	bhage
'we/you/they ran'	'if you/he wishes to run'
muṛe	muṛe
'turned'	'turn'

184. $(X\tilde{e})_{v,\ opt,\ pl,\ I} \longleftrightarrow (X\tilde{e})_{v,\ opt,\ pl,\ III}$

cəlẽ	cəlẽ
'we should go'	'they should go'
bədlẽ	bədlẽ
'we should change'	'they should change'

185. $(Xa)_{v,\ perf,\ masc,\ sing,\ I} \longleftrightarrow (Xa)_{v,\ perf,\ masc,\ sing,\ IInh/III}$

Condition: X ends in a consonant.

cəla	cəla
'I walked'	'you/he walked'
bhaga	bhaga
'I ran'	'you/he ran'

186. $(Xa)_{v,\ perf,\ masc,\ sing,\ I/IInh} \longleftrightarrow (Xa)_{v,Ist\ caus/III\ intra\ (derived\ transitive)}$

cəla	cəla
'I/you/he/walked'	'make somebody/something
uṭha	uṭha
'got up'	'lift'

187. $(Xna)_{v.\ nh.\ sing} \longleftrightarrow (Xna)_{v.\ hon}$

cəlna	cəlna
'you (sing) walk'	'you walk'
bhagna	bhagna
'you (sing) run'	'you run'

188. $(Xya)_{v.\ perf.\ masc.\ sing.\ I} \longleftrightarrow (Xya)_{v.\ perf.\ masc.\ sing.\ IInh/III}$

Condition: X ends in a vowel.

roya	roya
'I wept'	'you/he wept'
soya	soya
'I slept'	'you/he slept'

189. $(Xti)_{v.\ imperf.\ contin.\ fem.\ sing.\ I} \longleftrightarrow (Xti)_{v.\ imperf.\ contin.\ fem.\ sing.\ IInh/III}$

cəlti	cəlti
'I had/would have come'	'you/she had/ would have come'
bhagti	bhagti
'I had/would have run'	'you/she had/ would have run'

190. $(Xte)_{v.\ imperf.\ contin.\ masc.\ pl.\ I} \longleftrightarrow (Xte)_{v.\ imperf.\ contin\ masc.\ pl.\ II/III}$

khelte	khelte
'we had/would have played'	'you/they had/ would have played'
rote	rote
'had/would have cried'	'had/would have cried'

191. $(Xta)_{v.\ imperf.\ contin.\ masc.\ sing.\ I} \longleftrightarrow (Xta)_{v.\ imperf.\ contin.\ sing.\ masc.\ IInh/III}$

cəlta	cəlta
'I had/would have gone'	'you/he'd would have gone/
lıkhta	lıkhta
'had /would have written'	'had /would have written'

192. (Xtĩ)$_{\text{v, imperf, contin, fem, pl, I}}$ ⟷ (Xtĩ)$_{\text{v, imperf, contin, fem, pl, II/III}}$

kheltĩ	kheltĩ
'we had/would have played'	'you/they had/would have played'
cəltĩ	cəltĩ
'walked'	'walked'

193. (Xɪye)$_{\text{v, h, sing}}$ ⟷ (Xɪye)$_{\text{v, h, pl}}$

sunɪye	sunɪye
'you (hon, sing) listen'	'you (hon, pl) listen'
khelɪye	khelɪye
'you (hon, sing)play'	'you (hon, pl) play'

194. (Xegi)$_{\text{v, fut, fem, sing, III}}$ ⟷ (Xegi)$_{\text{v, fut, fem, sing, IInh}}$

khelegi	khelegi
'she will play'	'you (non-hon) will play'
gɪnegi	gɪnegi
'she will count'	'you (non-hon) count'

195. (Xẽgi)$_{\text{v, fut, fem, pl, I}}$ ⟷ (Xẽgi)$_{\text{v, fut, fem, pl, IIh/III}}$

lɪkhẽgi	lɪkhẽgi
'we will write'	'you/they will write'
kudẽgi	kudẽgi
'we will jump'	'you/they will jump'

196. (Xega)$_{\text{v, fut, masc, sing, III}}$ ⟷ (Xega)$_{\text{v, fut, masc, sing, IInh}}$

khelega	khelega
'he will play'	'you will play'
cəlega	cəlega
'he will walk'	'you will walk'

197. $(\text{Xɪyega})_{\text{v. fut. h. sing}} \longleftrightarrow (\text{Xɪyega})_{\text{v. fut. h. pl}}$

sunɪyega	sunɪyega
'you (sing) listen'	'you (pl) listen'
khelɪyega	khelɪyega
'you (sing) play'	'you (pl) play'

(b) *Suffixation* (WFSs 198-223)

198. $(\text{X})_{\text{v}} \longleftrightarrow (\text{Xi})_{\text{v, perf/pp, fem, sing, I/II nh, III}}$

cəl	cəli
'walk'	'I/you/she walked'
khel	kheli
'play'	'I/you/she played'

199. $(\text{X})_{\text{v}} \longleftrightarrow (\text{X}\tilde{\text{i}})_{\text{v, perf, fem, pl, I/II/III}}$

cəl	cəlĩ
'walk'	'we/you/they walked'
kud	kudĩ
'jump'	'we/you/they jumped'

200. $(\text{X})_{\text{v}} \longleftrightarrow (\text{Xe})_{\text{v, perf/pp, contin, masc, pl, I/II/III}}$

khel	khele
'play'	'we/you/they played'
bhag	bhage
'run'	'we/you/they ran'

201. $(\text{X})_{\text{v}} \longleftrightarrow (\text{Xe})_{\text{v, fut, contin, pl, I/ IIh/III}}$

mɪl	mɪle
'meet'	'if we/you/they meet'
lɪkh	lɪkhe
'write'	'if we/you/they write'

202. $(X)_v \longleftrightarrow (Xa)_{v,\ perf/pp\ masc,\ I/II\ (nh)/III,\ sing}$

Condition: X ends in a consonant.

cəl	cəla
'walk'	'I/you/he walked'
khel	khela
'play'	'I/you/he played'

203 $(X)_{v,\ intra} \longleftrightarrow (Xa)_{v,\ Ist\ caus\ (derived\ transitive)}$

Condition : X = PV̌C

gɪr	gɪra
'fall'	'fell'
cəl	cəla
'walk'	'drive'

204. $(X)_v \longleftrightarrow (Xa)_{v,\ IInd\ caus}$

ɖəs	ɖəsa
'bite'	'get A bitten by B (snake)'
lɪkh	lɪkha
'write'	'get written'

205. $(X)_v \longleftrightarrow (X\tilde{u})_{v,\ non\text{-}fut,\ opt,\ I,\ sing}$

khel	khelũ
'play'	'should I play?'
kha	khaũ
'eat'	'should I eat?'

206. $(X)_v \longleftrightarrow (Xo)_{v,\ imper,\ II}$

khel	khelo
'play'	'you play (*tʊm khelo*)'
lɪkh	lɪkho
'write'	'you write'

Note : Both the forms in WFS 206 are second person singular imperative (masc or fem). LHS form is used with II n-h *tʊ* whereas the RHS form is used with neutral *tʊm*. X*ɪye* form will be used with the II h *ap*.

207. $(X)_v \longleftrightarrow (Xti)_{pres\ p,\ imperf,\ fem}$

cəl	cəlti
'walk'	'walking'
bhag	bhagti
'run'	'running'

208. $(X)_v \longleftrightarrow (Xte)_{pres\ p,\ imperf,\ masc,\ pl}$

kha	khate
'eat'	'eating'
khel	khelte
'play'	'playing'

209. $(X)_v \longleftrightarrow (Xta)_{pres\ p,\ imperf,\ masc,\ sing}$

gɪn	gɪnta
'count'	'counting'
khel	khelta
'play'	'playing'

210. $(X)_v \longleftrightarrow (Xna)_{v,\ inf}$

kha	khana
'eat'	'to eat'
mar	marna
'beat'	'to beat'

211. $(X)_v \longleftrightarrow (Xva)_{v,\ IInd\ caus}$

gɪr	gɪrva
'fall'	'cause somebody else to fell'
lɪkh	lɪkhva
'write'	'cause somebody else to write'

Note : It is only in the case of *real activity* verbs that we can have two causal forms which are formally and semantically distinct. For example

	gɪr 'to fall'	pəɽh 'to study'
Ist casual	gɪra 'to fell'	pəɽha 'teach'
2nd causal	gɪrva 'to make somebody fell (e.g. a tree)	pəɽhva 'to get somebody taught'

In the case of reflexive verbs e.g. *pi* 'drink' where the action is directed toward the speàker, *-a* adjunction yields only a derived transitive e.g.

pi 'drink'
pɪla 'cause X to drink (action by subject)
pɪlva 'cause X to make somebody drink (causative)

In the case of transitive verbs, *-a* and *-va* adjunctions produce identical meanings e.g.

si	'stitch'
sɪla	'get stitched'
sɪlva	'get stitched by some body'

212. $(X)_v \longleftrightarrow (Xya)_{v,\ perf/pp,\ masc,\ sing,\ I/II\ nh/III}$

Condition: X ends in a vowel.

ro	roya
'cry'	'I/you/he cried'
so	soya
'sleep'	'I/you/he slept'

213. $(X)_v \longleftrightarrow (Xye)_{v,\ perf/pp,\ masc,\ pl,\ I/II\ nh}$

Condition: X ends in a vowel

ro	roye
'cry'	'we/you/they cried'
ghəbra	ghəbraye
'be nervous'	'we/you/they became nervous'

214. $(X)_v \longleftrightarrow (X\text{ɪye})_{v.\ imper.\ IIh}$

cəl	cəlɪye
'walk'	'you (h) walk'
kha	kharye
'eat'	'you (h) eat'

215. $(X)_v \longleftrightarrow (Xegi)_{v.\ fut.\ fem.\ sing.\ IInh\ III}$

mar	maregi
'beat'	'you (nh)she will beat'
khel	khelegi
'play'	'you (nh)/she will play'

216. $(X)_v \longleftrightarrow (X\tilde{e}gi)_{v.\ fut.\ fem.\ pl.\ I\ III.\ IIh}$

cʊn	cʊnẽgi
'select'	'we/they (fem) /you (h) will select'
ga	gaẽgi
'sing'	'we/they (fem)/you (h) will sing'

217. $(X)_v \longleftrightarrow (Xega)_{v.\ fut.\ masc.\ sing.\ II\ nh\ III}$

kud	kudega
'jump'	'you (nh)/he will jump
mar	marega
'beat'	'you (nh)/he will beat'

218. $(X)_v \longleftrightarrow (X\tilde{e}ge)_{v.\ fut.\ masc.\ pl.\ I\ III.IIh}$

bhag	bhagẽge
'run'	'we/they (masc)/you(h) will run
lɪkh	lɪkhẽge
'write'	'we/they(masc)/you(h) will write'

219. $(X)_v \longleftrightarrow (Xogi)_{v,\ fut,\ fem,\ II}$

khel	khelogi
'play'	'you (sing/pl) will play'
lɪkh	lɪkhogi
'write'	'you (sing/pl) will write'

220. $(X)_v \longleftrightarrow (Xoge)_{v,\ fut,\ masc,\ II}$

mar	maroge
'beat'	'you (sing/pl) will beat'
kha	khaoge
'eat'	'you (sing/pl) will eat'

221. $(X)_v \longleftrightarrow (X\tilde{u}gi)_{v,\ fut,\ fem,\ sing,\ I}$

bhag	bhagũi
'run'	'I (fem) will run'
khel	khelũgi
'play'	'I (fem) will play'

222. $(X)_v \longleftrightarrow (X\tilde{u}ga)_{v,\ fut,\ masc,\ sing,\ I}$

cəl	cəlũga
'walk'	'I (masc) will walk'
khel	khelũga
'play'	'I (masc) will play'

223 $(X)_v \longleftrightarrow$ (Xɪyega)$_{v,\ fut,\ IIh}$

bhag	bhagɪyega
'run'	'you (h) will run'
lɪkh	lɪkhɪyega
'write'	'you (h) will write'

(c) *Suffixation with morphophonemic changes* (WFSs 224-230)

224. $(PVC)_v \longleftrightarrow (P\check{V}Ca)_{v,\ Ist\ caus}$

bhag	bhəga
'run'	'make somebody run'
jit	jɪta
'win'	'get somebody to win'

225. $(PVQ)_{v} \longleftrightarrow (P\breve{V}Ca)_{v,\ \mathrm{IInd\ caus}}$

bhag	bhəgva
'run'	'make somebody/someone run'
ga	gəva
'sing'	'make somebody/someone sing'

226. $((P)C\underset{\substack{-\mathrm{high}\\+\mathrm{long}}}{V}C)_{v,tr} \longleftrightarrow ((P)C\underset{\substack{+\mathrm{high}\\-\mathrm{long}}}{\breve{V}}Ca)_{v,\ \mathrm{Ist\ caus}}$

khod	khʊda
'dig'	'get dug'
gher	ghɪra
'encircle'	'get encircled'

227. $((P)C\underset{\substack{-\mathrm{high}\\+\mathrm{long}}}{\breve{V}}(c))_{v} \longleftrightarrow ((P)C\ \underset{\substack{+\mathrm{high}\\-\mathrm{long}}}{\breve{V}}\ (c)\ la)_{v,\ \mathrm{Ist\ caus}}$

so	sʊla
'sleep'	'put somebody to sleep'
ro	rʊla
'cry'	'make somebody cry'
de	dɪla
'give'	'get'
dekh	dɪkhla
'see'	'show'

228 $((P)C\underset{\substack{-\mathrm{high}\\+\mathrm{long}}}{V}C)_{v} \longleftrightarrow ((P)C\underset{\substack{+\mathrm{high}\\-\mathrm{long}}}{V}Cva)_{v,\ \mathrm{IInd\ caus}}$

khel	khɪlva
'play'	'get something played'
khol	khʊlva
'open'	'get something opened'

229. $(C\underset{\substack{-high\\+long}}{V})_{v} \longleftrightarrow (C\underset{\substack{+high\\-long}}{V}lva)_{v,\ IInd\ caus}$

so	sʊlva
'sleep'	'get somebody to put somebody to sleep'
de	dɪlva
'give'	'get somebody to give somebody something'

230. $(PV)_{v} \longleftrightarrow (P\breve{V}lva)_{v,\ IInd\ caus}$

ji	jɪlva
'come to life'	'get A to bring B to life'
kha	khɪlva
'eat'	'get A to make B eat'

(d) *Substitution* (WFS 231)

231. $(Pa)_{v,\ tr} \longleftrightarrow (Pva)_{v,\ IInd\ caus}$

kəma	kəmva
'earn'	'get earned'
səta	sətva
'tease'	'get somebody teased'

(e) *Morphophonemic change* (WFSs 232-234)

232. $((P)C\breve{V}C)_{v,\ intr} \longleftrightarrow ((P)CVC)_{v,\ tr}$

sʊdhər	sʊdhar
'(you) improve'	'reform somebody else'
ʊtər	ʊtar
'get down'	'bring down (unload)'
pɪʈ	piʈ
'get beaten'	'beat (somebody)'
lʊʈ	luʈ
'get robbed'	'rob (somebody)'

233. $((P)C\underset{\substack{+high\\-long}}{V}C)_{v,\ intr} \longleftrightarrow ((P)C\underset{\substack{-high\\+long}}{V}C)_{v,\ tr}$

rʊk	rok
'stop'	'stop somebody'
mʊɽ	moɽ
'turn'	'turn something'
dɪkh	dekh
'appear'	'see'

234. $(C\breve{V}C)_{v,\ intr} \longleftrightarrow (C\tilde{V}\ C)_{v,\ tr}$

khɪc	khĩc
'get pulled'	'pull'
sɪc	sĩc
'get irrigated'	'irrigate'

8.6 *Verbs and Adjectives* (F)

(a) *Suffixation* (WFSs 235-249)

235. $(X)_v \longleftrightarrow (Xi)_{adj.\ fem}$

Condition: X does not end in -i or -u.

kha	khai
'eat'	'eaten'
so	soi
'sleep'	'sleeping'
cəl	cəli
'walk'	'walked'

236. $(X)_v \longleftrightarrow (Xe)_{adj.\ masc,\ pl}$

jəl	jəle
'burn'	'burnt'
kha	khae
'eat'	'eaten'

237. $(X)_v \longleftrightarrow (Xa)_{adj}$

Condition: X ends in a consonant.

cəl	cəla
'walk'	'walked'
jəl	jəla
'burn'	'burnt'

238. $(X)_v \longleftrightarrow (Xu)_{adj}$

Condition: X ends in -a.

kəma	kəmau
'earn'	'earning'
kha	khau
'eat'	'glutton'

239. $(X)_v \longleftrightarrow (Xau)_{adj}$

Condition : X ends in a consonant.

bık	bıkau
'sell'	'for sale'
cəl	cəlau
'walk'	'workable'

240. $(X)_v \longleftrightarrow (Xti)_{adj,\ fem}$

kha	khati
'eat'	'eating'
bhag	bhagti
'run'	'running'

241. $(X)_v \longleftrightarrow (Xte)_{adj,\ masc,\ pl}$

ro	rote
'cry'	'crying'
pi	pite
'drink'	'drinking'

242. $(X)_v \longleftrightarrow (Xta)_{adj,\ masc,\ sing}$

bhag	bhagta
'run'	'running'
so	sota
'sleep'	'sleeping'

243. $(X)_v \longleftrightarrow (Xvĩ)_{adj,\ fem}$

cʊn	cʊnvĩ
'select'	'selected'
jʊɽ	jʊɽvĩ
'attach'	'twin'

244. $(X)_v \longleftrightarrow (Xvã)_{adj,\ masc}$

jʊɽ	jʊɽvã
'attach'	'twins'
cʊn	cʊnvã
'select'	'selected'

245. $(X)_v \longleftrightarrow (Xya)_{adj,\ masc}$

Condition: X does not end in -i or -u.

kho	khoya
'lose'	'lost'
so	soya
'sleep'	'sleeping'

246 $(X)_v \longleftrightarrow (Xila)_{adj}$

səj	səjila
'decorate'	'decorated'
ḍəs	ḍəsila
'bite'	'poisnous'

247 $(X)_{v} \longleftrightarrow (X\text{ɪya})_{adj}$

ghəʈ	ghəʈɪya
'reduced'	'bad'
bəɽh	bəɽhɪya
'increase'	'good'

248. $(X)_{v} \longleftrightarrow (X\text{ɪyəl})_{adj}$

səɽ	səɽɪyəl
'decay'	'rotten'
əɽ	əɽɪyəl
'resist'	'obstinate'

249. $(X)_{v} \longleftrightarrow (X\text{vəni})_{adj.\ fem}$

ɖəra	ɖəravəni
'scare'	'fearful'
lʊbha	lʊbhavəni
'attract'	'attractive'

(b) *Suffixation with morphophonemic change* (WFSs 250-251)

250. $(PV)_{v} \longleftrightarrow (P\check{V}ya)_{adj.\ masc}$

pi	pɪya
'drink'	'drunk'
si	sɪya
'stitch'	'stitched'

251. $(PVQ)_{v} \longleftrightarrow (P\check{V}\,Q\text{əkkəɽ})_{adj.}$

ghum	ghʊməkkəɽ
'roam about'	'roaming'
bhul	bhʊləkkəɽ
'forget'	'forgetful'

(c) *Substitution* (WFSs 252 - 253)

252. $(Pu)_{v} \longleftrightarrow (P\upsilon a)_{adj.\ masc}$

cu	cʊa
'drip'	'drained'
chu	chʊa
'touch'	'touched'

253. $(Pu)_{v} \longleftrightarrow (P\upsilon i)_{adj.\ fem}$

chu	chʊi
'touch'	'touched'
cu	cʊi
'drip'	'drained'

8.7 *Verbs and Adverbs* (G)

(a) *Suffixation* (WFSs 254-258)

254. $(X)_{v} \longleftrightarrow (Xe)_{adv}$

cah	cahe
'wish'	'wishing'
bæṭh	bæṭhe
'sit'	'sitting'

255. $(X)_{v} \longleftrightarrow (Xti)_{adv.\ fem}$

bol	bolti
'speak'	'speaking'
bhag	bhagti
'run'	'running'

256. $(X)_{v} \longleftrightarrow (Xte)_{adv.\ pl}$

mar	marte
'beat'	'beating'
ro	rote
'cry'	'crying'

257. $(X)_v \longleftrightarrow (Xta)_{adv, masc}$

dɔɽ	dɔɽta
'run'	'running'
bhag	bhagta
'run'	'running'

258. $(X)_v \longleftrightarrow (Xkər)_{adv}$

dɔɽ	dɔɽkər
'run'	'running'
ʊʈh	ʊʈhkər
'get up'	'getting up'

8.8 *Adjectives and Adjectives* (H)

(a) *Identity* (WFS 259)

259. $(X)_{adj, masc} \longleftrightarrow (X)_{adj, fem}$

lal	lal
'red'	'red'
bɪkau	bɪkau
'for sale'	'for sale'

(b) *Suffixation* (WFSs 260-261)

260. $(X)_{adj} \longleftrightarrow (Xtər)_{adj, comp}$

ədhɪk	ədhɪktər
'more'	'more'
koməl	koməltər
'soft'	'softer'

261. $(X)_{adj} \longleftrightarrow (Xtəm)_{adj, super}$

sʊndər	sʊndərtəm
'beautiful'	'most beautiful'
nɪkəʈ	nɪkəʈtəm
'near'	'nearest'

(c) *Prefixation* (WFS 262)

262. $(X)_{adj} \longleftrightarrow (məhaX)_{adj.\ inten}$

ḍərpok	məhaḍərpok
'coward'	'extremely coward'
bhəyanək	məhabhəyanək
'terrifying'	'extremely terrifying'

(d) *Substitution* (WFSs 263-264)

263. $(Pa)_{adj.\ masc.\ sing} \longleftrightarrow (Pi)_{adj.\ fem}$

moṭa	moṭi
'fat'	'fat'
bəṛa	bəṛi
'big'	'big'

264. $(Pa)_{adj.\ masc.\ sing} \longleftrightarrow (Pe)_{adj.\ masc.\ pl}$

ləmba	ləmbe
'long'	'long'
bəṛa	bəṛe
'big'	'big'

(e) *Substitution with morphophonemic change* (WFS 265)

265. $(Pvi)_{adj.\ masc} \longleftrightarrow (Pvɪni)_{adj.\ fem}$

mayavi	mayavɪni
'deceitful'	'deceitful'
medhavi	medhavɪni
'wise'	'wise'

8.9 *Adjectives and Adverbs* (I)

(a) *Suffixation* (WFSs 266 - 269)

266. $(X)_{adj} \longleftrightarrow (Xən)_{adv}$

kərib	kəribən
'near'	'almost'

məjbur	məjburən
'helpless'	'perforce'

267. $(X)_{adj} \longleftrightarrow (Xtər)_{adv}$

Condition: X has an element of frequency.

ədhık	ədhıktər
'more'	'generally'
jyada	jyadatər
'more'	'generally'

268. $(X)_{adj} \longleftrightarrow (Xkər)_{adv}$

xas	xaskər
'special'	'specially'
vıšeš	vıšeškər
'special'	'specially'

269. $(X)_{adj} \longleftrightarrow (Xtəya)_{adv}$

purṇ	purṇtəya
'complete'	'completely'
sadharəṇ	sadharəṇtəya
'ordinary'	'ordinarily'

(B) *Substitution* (WFS 270)

270. $(Pa)_{adj} \longleftrightarrow (Pe)_{adv}$

əkela	əkele
'single'	'all by oneself'
dusra	dusre
'second'	'secondly'

8.10 *Adverbs*

There is no intracategorial WFSs relating adverbs to other adverbs. Adverbs in MH are either invariant or related to nouns, verbs and adjectives.

8.11 *Dormant Strategies*

Intra- and Intercategorial

A. *Nouns*

DS 1 (dɪl)$_{\text{n. masc. sing}}$ ⟷ (dɪler)$_{\textit{n.}\text{ masc. sing.}}$ *having* X
'heart' 'courageous'

DS2 (pʊl)$_{\text{n. masc. sing}}$ ⟷ (pʊlɪya)$_{\text{n. masc. sing.}}$ *small* X
'bridge ' 'small bridge'

DS3 (bat)$_{\text{n. fem. sing}}$ ⟷ (batuni)$_{\text{n. masc. sing}}$
'talk' 'talkative'

DS4 (rəŋ)$_{\text{n. masc. sing}}$ ⟷ (rəŋrez)$_{\text{n. masc. sing}}$
'colour' 'one who colours

DS5 (dəst)$_{\text{n. masc. sing}}$ ⟷ (dəstavez)$_{\text{n. masc. pl}}$
'hand' 'documents'

DS6 (nak)$_{\text{n. fem. sing}}$ ⟷ (nəkel)$_{\text{n. fem. sing}}$
'nose' 'hatter-pin'

DS7 (hath)$_{\text{n. masc. sing}}$ ⟷ (həthɔɽa)$_{\text{n. masc. sing}}$
'hand' 'hammer'

DS8 (bag)$_{\text{n. masc. sing}}$ ⟷ (bəgica)$_{\text{n. masc. sing}}$
'garden' 'small garden'

DS9 (həjjam)$_{\text{n. masc. sing}}$ ⟷ (həjamət)$_{\text{n. fem. sing}}$
'barber ' 'shave'

DS10 (khaj)$_{\text{n. fem. sing}}$ ⟷ (khʊjli)$_{\text{n. fem. sing}}$
'itch' 'itchiness'

DS11 (bap)$_{\text{n. masc. sing}}$ ⟷ (bəpɔti)$_{\text{n. fem. sing}}$
'father' 'inheritance'

DS12 (pãv)$_{\text{n. masc. sing}}$ ⟷ (payəl)$_{\text{n. fem. sing}}$
'foot' 'anklet with bells'

DS13 (bãs)$_{\text{n. masc. sing}}$ ⟷ (bãsʊri)$_{\text{n. fem. sing}}$
'bamboo' 'flute'

DS14 (bat)$_{\text{n. fem. sing}}$ ⟷ (bətəŋgəɽ)$_{\text{n. masc. sing}}$
'talk, issue 'issue blown out of proportion

DS15 (bhap)$_{\text{n. fem. sing}}$ ⟷ (bəphara)$_{\text{n. masc. sing}}$
'steam' 'vapour'

DS16 (ɖɪbba)$_{\text{n. masc. sing}}$ ⟷ (dɪbɪya)$_{\text{n. fem. sing}}$
'box' 'small box'

DS17 (luʈ)$_{\text{n. masc. sing}}$ ⟷ (lʊʈera)$_{\text{n. masc. sing}}$
'loot' 'robber'

DS18 (gʊɖɖa)$_{\text{n. masc. sing}}$ ⟷ (gʊɽɪya)$_{\text{n. fem. sing}}$
'doll' 'doll'

DS19 (bhai)$_{\text{n. masc. sing}}$ ⟷ (bhətija)$_{\text{n. masc. sing}}$
'brother' 'nephew' (brother's son)

DS20 (bəhɪn)$_{\text{n. sing. fem}}$ ⟷ (bhanja)$_{\text{n. masc. sing}}$
'sister' 'nephew' (sister's son)

DS21 (khel)$_{\text{n. masc. sing}}$ ⟷ (khɪlaɽi)$_{\text{n. masc. sing}}$
'game' 'player'

DS22 (put)$_{\text{n. masc. sing}}$ ⟷ (kəput)$_{\text{n. masc. sing}}$
'son' 'bad son'

DS23 (gʊṇ)$_{\text{n. masc. sing}}$ ⟷ (əvgʊṇ)$_{\text{n. masc. sing}}$
'quality' 'weakness'

DS24 (rag)$_{\text{n. masc. sing}}$ ⟷ (bærag)$_{\text{n. masc.sing}}$
'attachment' 'detachment'

DS25 (məsti)$_{\text{n. fem. sing}}$ ⟷ (əlməsti)$_{\text{n. fem. sing}}$
'joy' 'great joy'

DS26 (kəh)$_{\text{v}}$ ⟷ (kəhani)$_{\text{n. fem. sing}}$
'say' 'story'

DS27 (bəs)$_{\text{v}}$ ⟷ (bəsera)$_{\text{n. masc. sing}}$
'settle down' 'lodging'

DS28 (dhər)$_{\text{v}}$ ⟷ (dhərohər)$_{\text{n. fem. sing}}$
'keep' 'something entrusted'

DS29 (nɪpəʈ)$_{\text{v}}$ ⟷ (nɪpʈara)$_{\text{n. masc. sing}}$
'resolve' 'resolution'

DS30 (khʊja)$_{\text{v}}$ ⟷ (khʊjli)$_{\text{n. fem. sing}}$
'scratch' 'itch'

DS31 (jhul)$_{\text{v}}$ ⟷ (jhol)$_{\text{n. masc. sing}}$
'swing' 'wavy'

DS32 (jəm)$_{\text{v}}$ ⟷ (jamən)$_{\text{n. masc. sing}}$
'set (curd)' 'rennet'

DS33 $(\text{mɪl})_{v}$ ⟷ $(\text{mɪlap})_{n, masc, sing}$
'meet' 'union'

DS34 $(\text{tær})_{v}$ ⟷ $(\text{tærak})_{n, masc, sing}$
'swim' 'swimmer'

DS35 $(\text{hɪl})_{v}$ ⟷ $(\text{hɪlor})_{n, fem, sing}$
'move' 'ripple'

DS36 $(\text{rəkh})_{v}$ ⟷ $(\text{rəkhæl})_{n, fem, sing}$
'keep' 'mistress'

DS37 $(\text{pila})_{adj}$ ⟷ $(\text{pilɪya})_{n, masc, sing}$
'yellow' 'jaundice'

DS38. $(\text{bənd})_{adj}$ ⟷ $(\text{bəndɪš})_{n, fem, sing}$
'closed' 'restriction'

DS39. $(\text{zərur})_{adv}$ ⟷ $(\text{zərurət})_{n, fem, sing}$
'certainly' 'need'

B. *Verbs*

DS40 $(\text{phəʈ})_{v, intr}$ ⟷ $(\text{phaɽ})_{v, tr}$
'get torn' 'tear'

DS41 $(\text{bɪk})_{v, intr}$ ⟷ $(\text{bec})_{v, tr}$
'get sold' 'sell'

DS42 $(\text{sɪla})_{v,intr}$ ⟷ $(\text{si})_{v, tr}$
'get stitched' 'stitch'

DS43 $(\text{dhʊl})_{v, intr}$ ⟷ $(\text{dho})_{v, tr}$
'get washed' 'wash'

DS44 $(\text{ʈuʈ})_{v, intr}$ ⟷ $(\text{toɽ})_{v, tr}$
'get broken' 'break'

DS45 $(\text{sukh})_{v, intr}$ ⟷ $(\text{sokh})_{v, tr}$
'get dried' 'dry'

C. *Adjectives*

DS46 $(\text{baki})_{adj}$ ⟷ $(\text{bəkaya})_{adj}$
'remaining' 'remaining'

DS47 $(\text{nəv})_{adj}$ ⟷ $(\text{nəvin})_{adj}$
'new' 'new'

DS48 $(\text{məst})_{adj} \longleftrightarrow (\text{əlməst})_{adj}$
'happy' 'very happy'

DS49 $(\text{ghər})_{n,\ masc,\ sing} \longleftrightarrow (\text{ghərelu})_{adj}$
'home' 'homely'

DS50 $(\text{šok})_{n,\ masc,\ sing} \longleftrightarrow (\text{šocniy})_{adj}$
'mourning' 'lamentable'

DS51 $(\text{dʊnɪya})_{n,\ fem,sing} \longleftrightarrow (\text{dʊnɪyai})_{adj}$
'world' 'worldly'

DS52. $(\text{sərhana})_{n,\ fem,\ sing} \longleftrightarrow (\text{sərahniy})_{adj}$
'appreciation' 'appreciable'

DS53. $(\text{bat})_{n,fem,\ sing} \longleftrightarrow (\text{batuni})_{adj}$
'talk' 'talkative'

DS54 3$(\text{dɪl})_{n,\ masc,\ sing} \longleftrightarrow (\text{dɪler})_{adj}$
'heart' 'courageous'

DS55 $(\text{bəcca})_{n,\ masc,\ sing} \longleftrightarrow (\text{bəckana})_{adj}$
'child' 'child-like'

DS56 $(\text{ghɪn})_{n,\ fem,\ sing} \longleftrightarrow (\text{ghɪnɔna})_{adj}$
'repulsion' 'repulsive'

DS57. $(\text{rup})_{n,\ masc,\ sing} \longleftrightarrow (\text{rʊpəhla})_{adj}$
'beauty' 'beautiful'

DS58. $(\text{kajər})_{n,\ masc,\ sing} \longleftrightarrow (\text{kəjrai})_{adj}$
'black eye' 'cosmetic black (eyes)'

DS59 $(\text{jag})_{v} \longleftrightarrow (\text{jagrʊk})_{adj}$
'wake up' 'awakened'

DS60 $(\text{cʊn})_{v} \longleftrightarrow (\text{cʊnĩda})_{adj}$
'select' 'selected'

DS61. $(\text{ləɽ})_{v} \longleftrightarrow (\text{ləɽaku})_{adj}$
'fight' 'quarrelsome'

DS62 $(\text{jəldi})_{adv} \longleftrightarrow (\text{jəldbaz})_{adj}$
'quickly' 'quick'

D. *Adverbs*

DS63 $(\text{roz})_{adv} \longleftrightarrow (\text{rozana})_{adv}$
'daily' 'daily'

DS64. $(\text{əgər})_{adv} \longleftrightarrow (\text{əgərce})_{adv}$
'if' 'if'

CHAPTER 9

MORPHOLOGICAL NETWORKS

9.0 Introduction

Based on the theory presented in Chapter 3, conventions and heuristic devices discussed in Chapter 7 and the description of Hindi WFSs in Chapter 8, we present in this chapter a sample of possible morophological networks in Hindi. This is rather a naive, though theoretically and empirically well-motivated, approximation to the architecture of word-relatedness in the human mind. The empirical foundations are located in the description in Chapter 8. The high level of redundancy in the WFSs is counter-balanced by the fact that there are no exceptions to these strategies. We repeat that a speaker has multiple ways of accessing a particular word in her mental lexicon. We have no way of predicting which route will be utilized at a given point of time. We assume that all the routes get activated when a particular word is being accessed.

9.1 Nominal Networks

The most general cycle for singular nouns (except the masculine nouns ending in -a e.g. *ləɽka* 'boy') in Hindi is captured through a couple of WFSs involving identity. We could represent it as a network as in Fig 9.1 below :

Fig 9.1 : The general nominal cycle

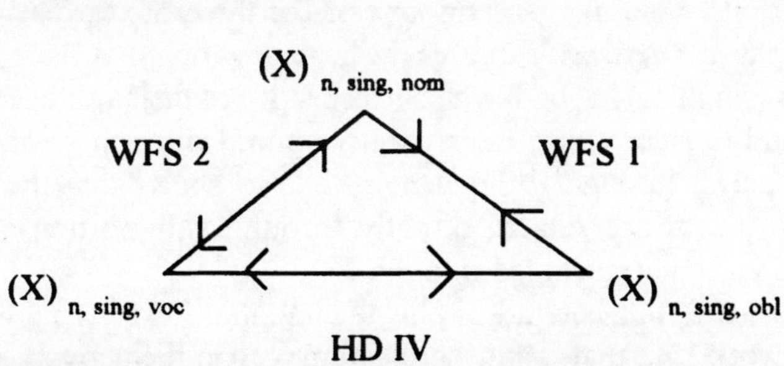

Of the six WFSs involved in this network only two need to be stated. The remaining four follow from the principle of bidirectionality and the Hueristic

Device IV. This network captures the empirical fact that except the *-a* ending masculine nouns, Hindi nouns in the singular remain invariant across different cases. This generalization of overwhelming importance may remain unnoticed in most traditional ways of handling word-relatedness.

Fig. 9.2 presents another simple network in nominal morphology involving two adjunction WFSs.

Fig. 9.2 : A simple nominal network

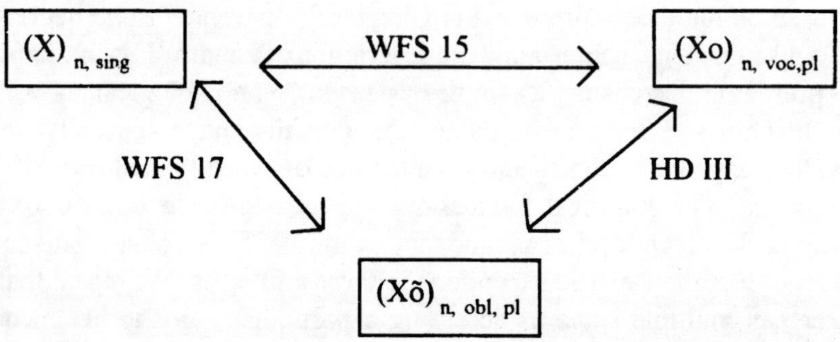

Condition: X does not end in -ɪ, -i, or -u. It also does not end in -a if X is masculine, honorific words excluded. X= *ghər, mala, rat, raja* etc.

It should be obvious that the network in Fig 9.1 can easily plug into the network in Fig 9.2 and create a more complex network . It is this process of chain plugging that will eventually lead us to an approximation of the ways in which the mental lexicon may be organized. There are really six WFSs involved here. The principle of bidirectionality has reduced them to three. Of these one does not need to be stated (see 7.2). Fig 9.1 reduces these six WFSs into one network. All the six strategies become accessible simultaneously the moment any one of the three boxes receives a signal. Notice that this network captures the generalization that there is a large set of nouns (singular) in Hindi which irrespective of their value for the features 'case' and 'gender' form their vocative plural through *-õ* adjunction and oblique plural through *-o* adjunction. It also shows that the oblique and vocative plural are related directly through substitution and that this relationship is not mediated through X.

In Fig. 9.3, this network is plugged into more WFSs and what emerges is a Network Unit that is far more complex than the network in Fig 9.2.

Fig.9.3: A network involving five related forms

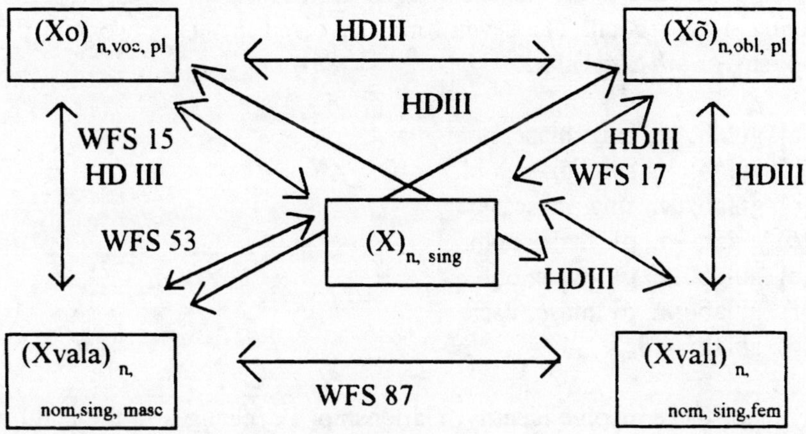

Since there are five related forms involved, twenty WFSs will be required to capture their relationship. In our description we have stated only four, namely, WFSs 15,17, 53 and 87. Others are subsumed by bidirectionality and heuristic devices. In the theory that motivates this description, there is nothing odd about, for example, obtaining

ghərvala 'house owner'
from ghərõ, 'houses' (obl, pl)

through a strategy of substitution though it can equally well be accessed through *ghəro, ghərvali* and *ghər*. The whole point of the network is that no form, simple or complex, has any privileged status. Computational ease is not our agenda. Human mind is indeed capable of handling phenomena of considerable complexity.

One may ask 'How does WFS 87 capture the relationship (Xvala) ~ (Xvali) ?' WFS 87 states the relationship (Pa) ~ (Pi) and has a structural description that fits (Xvala) ~ (Xvali). The *Xval* part of (Xvala) ~ (Xvali) is treated as P here. The relationship (X) ~ (Xvali) is captured by the *vice-versa* part of HD III.

We will of course have to continuously refine, modify and extend these networks. It should be clear from the condition given in Fig 9.2 that though *-vala* and *-vali* adjunction will apply for all singular nouns the *-o* and *-õ* adjunction will not apply if the noun ends in - ɪ, -i or -u.

For vocative and oblique plural forms in these cases we'll have to bring in WFSs 30, 31, 96 and 97 into the network.

We may extend the nominal network intercategorially. Fig. 9.4 (p.163) includes, in addition to the various nominal forms, related adjectival forms involving -i adjunction. The seven forms involved in this network in the case of say *gʊlab* 'rose' are :

(a) gʊlab: n, sing, masc, nom
(b) gʊlab: n, sing, masc, obl
(c) gʊlab: n, sing, masc, voc
(d) gʊlab: n, pl, masc, nom
(e) gʊlabõ: n, pl, masc, obl
(f) gʊlabo: n, pl, masc, voc
(g) gʊlabi: adj

Four of these involve identity relationship, i.e. changes in the feature matrix do not correspond to any formal marking. Each one of these words is accessible through six different paths (notice that each box has six arrowheads pointing at it). For example, the adjective. *gʊlabi* is directly accessed through *gʊlab* in (a) through *-i* adjunction. But it could equally well be accessed through all the other forms (b) to (f). *gulabi* is related to *gʊlabõ* and *gʊlabo* through strategies of substitution which follow from invoking Heuristic Device III once WFSs 15, 17 and 126 have been stated. In fact, for the 42 WFSs involved in Fig. 9.4 we actually state only 6 WFSs, namely, WFSs 1, 2, 3 (to capture relationships of identity) and 15, 17 and 126 (to capture relationships of adjunction). The thiry-six remaining WFSs follow from the implementation of Heuristic Devices II, III and IV.

Notice that the network does not make a distinction in terms of the processes involved, irrespective of whether the change is an intracategorial one of number, case or gender or an inter-categorial one e.g. from noun to adjective.

Fig 9.4 : An intra-and intercategorial nominal network

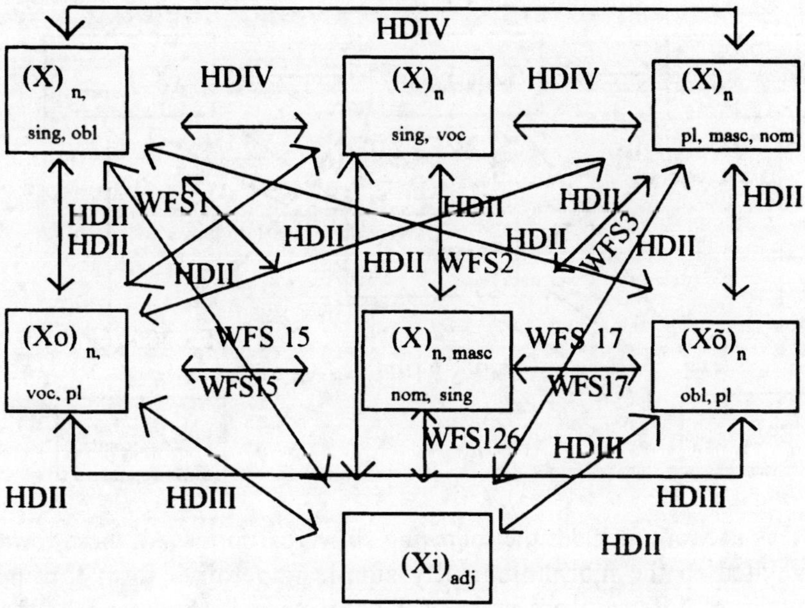

X = *gulab, lalэc, əŋgur , deš* etc.

9.2 *Complex Networks*

As we have already indicated, the simplest Hindi verbal network which does not include formal changes corresponding to changes in number, gender and person may be represented as follows (Fig 9.5 p.164).

Fig. 9.5 : Basic Verbal Network in Hindi.

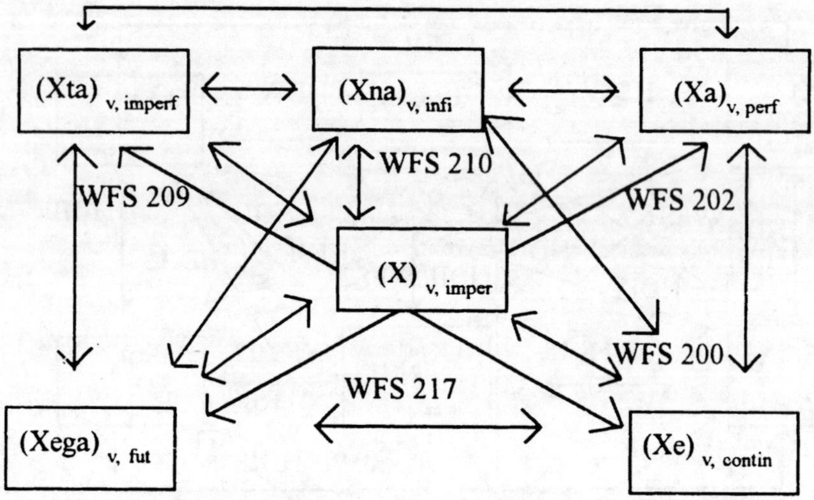

This network includes the following six verbal forms. All these forms are related to the morphologically simple imperative form through adjunction of different word-parts; each one of them is of course related to all the rest through substitution strategies subsumed by the Heuristic Device III.

(X)	:	v, imper	(cəl 'walk')
(Xa)	:	v, perf	(cəla 'walked', perfective aspect)
(Xe)	:	v, contin	(cəle 'walk', contingent mood)
(Xta)	:	v, imperf	(cəlta 'walks' imperfective aspect)
(Xna)	:	v, inf	(cəlna 'walk', infinitive)
(Xega)	:	v, fut	(cəlega 'will walk', future tense)

Thus the only tense marked in the Hindi main verb is the future; *-a* and *-ta* respectively mark the perfect and imperfect aspects; *-e* marks the contingent mood and *-na* the infinitive. Once again, the imperative form, though morphologically simple, has no privileged status. *cəlta* and *cəlna* are related in an equally straightforward way through a WFS of substitution.

In Fig 9.6 (p.165) we move towards a slightly more complex network. It is impossible to even visualize a full-blown network in a limited two-dimensional space. Only a high powered computer may provide some

Fig. 9.6 : An intra- and inter-categorial verbal network

(X = *cəl, sʊn, lɪkh*, etc.)

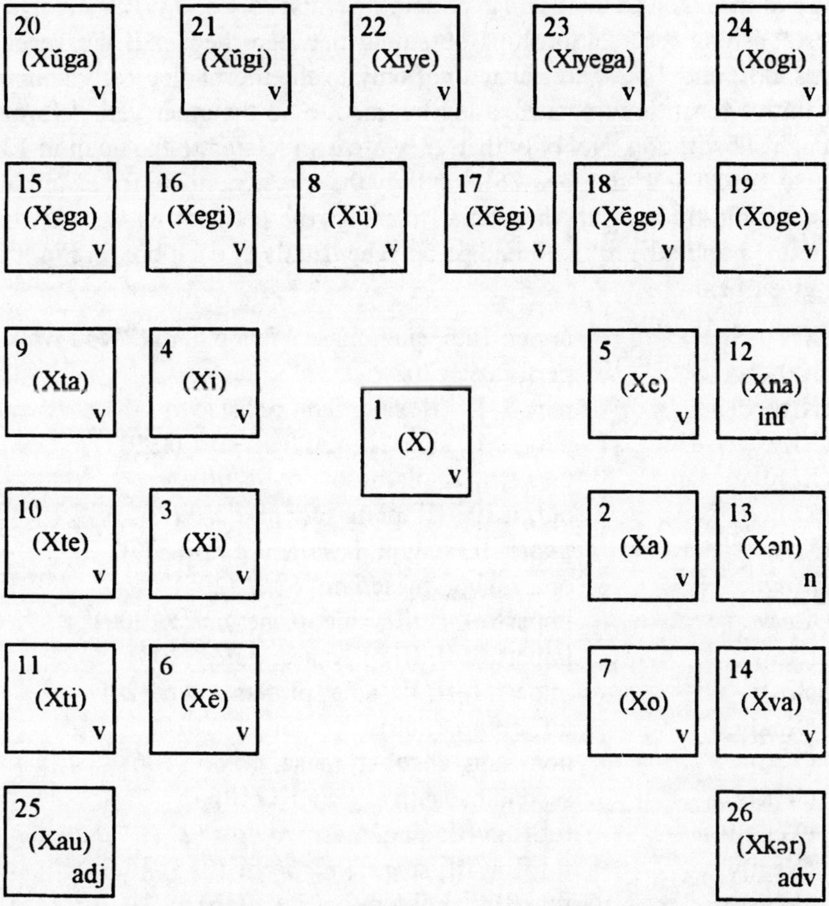

simulation of hundreds of relationships functioning simultaneously. The network in Fig. 9.6 is thus only partial. It does not even mark the relationships that are subsumed by different Heuristic Devices. Since there are 26 forms involved there will in principle be 26 x 25 = 650 WFSs involved in establishing the relationships obtaining between them. All the verbal forms 1-12 and 14-24 are related not only to the morphologically simple imperative form through suffixation but also to all the other verbal forms through substitution. Not only that, they are also related to the noun in 13, adjective in 25 and adverb in 26. Similarly the adjective in 25, for example, is accessible through all the verbal forms in the network as well as the noun in 13 and adverb in 26 and so on. The details of each box in Fig 9.6 are given below:

1. (X)v	:	imper, IInh, sing, masc / fem e.g. *cəl*. 'you walk'
2. (Xa)v	:	perf, *cəla* (202)
3. (Xi)v	:	perf, I, II, III, sing, fem, *cəli* (198)
4. (Xi)v	:	perf, I, II, sing, III, nh, fem; *cəli* (199)
5. (Xe)v	:	perf,I,II,III, pl, masc; *cəle* (200)
6. (Xẽ)v	:	opt, I, IIh, III, pl masc/fem; *cəlẽ* (201)
7. (Xo)v	:	imper, II, sing/pl,masc/fem *cəlo* (206)
8. (Xũ)v	:	opt, I, sing, masc/fem; *cəlũ* (205)
9. (Xta)v	:	imperf , I, II, III, sing, masc; *cəlta* (209)
10. (Xte)v	:	imperf, I, II, III, pl, masc; *cəlte* (208)
11. (Xti)v	:	imperf, I, II, III, sing, pl, fem; *cəlti* (207)
12. (Xna)v	:	inf; *cəlna* (209)
13. (Xən)n	:	nom sing, abstract, masc; *cələn* (106)
14. (Xva)v	:	second causative; *cəlva* (210)
15. (Xega)v	:	fut,IInh/III, sing, masc;*cəlega* (217)
16. (Xegi)v	:	fut,IInh/III, sing, fem;*cəlegi* (215)
17. (Xẽgi)v	:	fut,I/IIh/III,pl,fem;*cəlẽgi* (216)
18. (Xẽge)v	:	fut, I/III, pl, masc; *cəlẽge* (218)
19. (Xoge)v	:	fut,II, sing/pl,masc;*cəloge* (220)
20. (Xũga)v	:	fut, I, sing,masc; *cəlũga* (220)
21. (Xũgi)v	:	fut, I, sing fem; *cəlũgi* (221)
22. (Xɪye)v	:	imper, IIh, sing/pl, masc/fem; *cəlɪye* (214)
23. (Xɪyega)v	:	fut, IIh, sing/pl, masc/fem; *cəlɪyega* (223)
24. (Xogi)v	:	fut,IIh/III, sing, fem; *cəlogi* (219)
25. (Xau)adj	:	masc/fem; *cəlau* (239)
26. (Xkər)adv	:	*cəlkər* (258)

CHAPTER 10

INTERPRETATIONS AND CONCLUSIONS

10.0 *Introduction*

The 270 WFSs presented in Chapter 8 may be regarded as the basic strategies that capture the phenomena of word-relatedness in Modern Hindi. The number of these strategies will of course multiply manifold once the heuristic devices discussed in Chapter 7 are also invoked. Each WFS consists of an LHS and an RHS neither of which has any privileged status because of the bidirectional nature of the morphological operation involved. Each WFS plugs into a variety of WFSs depending on the structural description associated with them and the set of words on which they are based. The description thus makes each word accessible through a variety of paths in the extremely complex network we attempt to capture with these WFSs and the heuristic devices listed in Chapter 7. We have also listed 64 Dormant Strategies any one of which is likely to get activated and become the basis of a new WFS as and when another pair of words belonging to that dormant strategy is identified to make an analysis in terms of words and word-parts possible.

10.1 *Intra- and Intercategorial Operations*

Of the 270 WFSs, 165 (61.11%) account for intracategorial relationships while the remaining 105 (38.89%) for intercategorial ones (Table 10.1 p.168). Obviously, there is lot more happening within a grammatical category in Hindi than across. Straightforward suffixation, which involves no internal phonic modification, is the most favourite device used both intra- and intercategorially. More than half (52.96%) the WFSs in Hindi involve this type of suffixation; over 44% category-internal changes are achieved through suffixation while over 65% changes across grammatical categories also involve straightfordward suffixation. If we include both suffixation and prefixation under 'adjunction', intracategorial adjunction proportion will rise to above 59% and the intercategorial one above 74%. Identity figures next as a morphological process both intra- and intercategorially. It accounts for about 15% of the total WFSs. It is far more important intra- (18.18%) than inter- (9.52%) categorially. Substitution is fairly evenly distributed and accounts for over 8% of the WFSs.

Table 10.1 Percentage proportions of different morphological operations intra- and inter-categorially

	Intracategorial	Intercategorial	Total
(a) Identity	30 (18.18)	10 (9.52)	40 (14.8)
(b) Suffixation	74 (44.84)	69 (65.71)	143 (52.96)
(c) Suffixation with morphophonemic change	15 (9.09)	5 (4.76)	20 (7.78)
(d) Prefixation	26 (15.76)	10 (9.52)	36 (13.33)
(e) Prefixation with morphophonemic change	-	-	-
(f) Substitution	16 (9.70)	6 (5.71)	22 (8.15)
(g) Substitution with morphophonemic change	1 (.61)	2 (1.90)	3 (1.11)
(h) Deletion	- -	1 (.95)	1 (.37)
(i) Deletion with morphophonemic change	- -	2 (1.90)	2 (.74)
(J) Morphophonemic change	3 (1.18)	-	3 (1.11)
	165 (61.11)	105 (38.89)	270 (100.00)

Table 10.2 Intracategorial Word Formation Strategies (n=165)
(Numbers in parenthesis indicate the WFS numbers in Chapter 8)

Morphological operation	Nouns 8.1(A)	Verbs 8.5(E)	Adjectives 8.8(H)	Adverbs 8.10(J)	Total
(a) Identity	7 (1-7)	22 (176-197)	1 (259)	–	30
(b) Suffixation	46 (8-53)	26 (189-223)	2 (260-261)	–	74
(c) Suffixation with morphophonemic change	8 (54-61)	7 (224-230)	–	–	15
(d) Prefixation	25 (62-86)	– –	1 (261)	– –	26
(e) Prefixation with morphophonemic change	–	–	–	–	
(f) Substitution	13 (87-99)	1 (231)	2 (263-264)	– –	16
(g) Substitution with morphophonemic change	–	–	1 (265)	–	1
(h) Deletion	–	3 (232-234)			3
Total	99	59	7	–	165

Table 10.3 Intercategorial Word Formation Strategies (n=105) (WFS numbers correspond to Chapter 8)

Morphological operation	n↔v 8.2(B)	n↔adj 8.3(C)	n↔adv 8.4(D)	v↔adj 8.6(F)	v↔adv 8.7(G)	adj↔adv 8.9(I)	Total
Identity	2	8	-	-	-	-	10
WFS Nos.	100-101	118-125					
Suffixation	13	29	3	15	5	4	69
WFS Nos.	102-114	126-154	169-170	235-249	254-258	266-269	
Suffixation with morphophonemic change	-	3	-	2	-	-	5
WFS Nos.		155-157		250-251			
Prefixation	-	6	4	-	-	-	10
WFS Nos.		158-163	171-174				
Prefixation with morphophonemic change							
WFS Nos.	-	-	-	-	-	-	-
Substitution	-	2	1	2	-	1	6
WFS Nos.		164-165	175	252-253		270	
Substitution with morphophonemic change	-	2	-	-	-	-	2
WFS Nos.		166-167					
Deletion	1						1
WFS No	115	-	-	-	-	- -	
Deletion with morphophonemic change	2						2
WFS Nos.	116-117	-	-	-	-	-	
Morphophonemic change	-	-	-	-	-	-	-
Total	18	50	8	19	5	5	105

MH does not make an extensive use of morphophonemic change as a morphological device either by itself or in combination with adjunction, substitution or deletion. Morphophonemic change by itself is indeed used very sparingly (about 1% of the times and only intracategorially). Nor is it used with any noticeable frequency in combination with substitution or deletion. It is only with suffixation that morphophonemic changes appear (about 9% of the times intra- and about 5% of the times inter-categorially). We will return to these cases of double-marking in a later section. We should, however, like to repeat that even in these cases the morphophonemic change is inseparable from the affixes in question.

10.2 *Adverbs*

Table 10.2 provides us a breakdown of the intracategorial MH morphology. We notice that MH adverbs are largely invariant and there are no morphological operations that relate adverbs to other adverbs. In fact, there is a very limited inter-categorial adverbial morphology either (Table 10.3). There are only 18 WFSs that relate adverbs to nouns (8), verbs (5) and adjectives (5). These WFSs generally involve suffixation (12 out of 18) as is, for example, the case with the four WFSs 266-269 involving adjectives and adverbs of frequency, periodicity or specificity. Again all the five WFSs 254-258 that describe the relationships obtaining between verbs and adverbs involve suffixation. These suffixation strategies result in '-ing' type adverbs.

10.3 *Adjectives*

Intracategorial adjectival morphology is also very limited in MH. There are only 7 WFSs which relate adjectives to other adjectives (cf. Table 10.2). These WFSs may be seen in section 8.8 (WFSs 259-265). The fact that MH has a set of so-called 'red' adjectives which remain invariant when there are gender and number changes in the following noun is captured by the following WFS

259. $(X)_{\text{adj, masc}} \longleftrightarrow (X)_{\text{adj, fem}}$

Since the feature number is not specified on either side, this WFS involving identity is true for both singular and plural adjectives. The relationships obtaining among the adjectives in the so-called 'black' set (e.g. *kala* 'black', *ləmba* 'long', *moṭa* 'fat' etc.) which change their form depending on the gender and number of the following noun is captured by the two substitution WFSs given below:

263. $(Pa)_{adj, masc, sing} \longleftrightarrow (Pi)_{adj, fem}$

264. $(Pa)_{adj, masc, sing} \longleftrightarrow (Pe)_{adj, masc, pl}$

Notice that we use the variable 'P' and not 'X' here because P is only a 'word part' and not a word. Only 'Pa' or 'Pi' or 'Pe' constitutes a word. In WFS 263, feature number is left unspecified because the feminine adjectives *kali, ləmbi, moṭi* etc. remain invariant across number in the case of feminine nouns. The variation in the case of masculine nouns is captured by WFS 264. The relationship

$(Pi)_{adj, fem} \longleftrightarrow (Pe)_{adj, masc, pl}$

which is indeed central to the network model of morphology will be captured by one of our Heuristic Devices, namely HD IV. The comparative and superlative adjectives are related to simple adjectives in WFSs 260-261 and the relationship *Xṭər-Xṭəm* will be activated by invoking a Heuristic Device, namely, HD III.

There is a fairly rich intercategorial adjectival morphology. There are 50 WFSs that relate nouns and adjectives and 19 WFSs that relate verbs and adjectives (Table 10.3). Over 63% of these WFSs, involve suffixation without any morphophonemic changes. There are many nouns in MH which can also be used as adjectives but there are no identity relationships obtaining between MH verbs and adjectives. Masculine nouns ending in *-i*, *-baz*, *-vər*, *-var*, *-van*, *-mənd*, *-əsvi* and *-əndaz* (see WFSs 118-125 in 8.3) can also be used as adjectives. Prefixation (WFSs 158-163)and substitution (WFSs 164-165) are also often used to capture the relatedness between nouns and adjectives in MH. Adjective forming prefixation is used on nouns largely to achieve the meaning of 'opposite of X', the noun prefixes e.g. *ə-*, *nɪ-*, *la-*, *nɪr-*, and *nɪš-* as in *əkal* 'untimely', *nɪḍər* 'fearless', *laɪlaj* 'incurable', *nɪrəstr* 'unarmed' and *nɪškam* 'detached' form adjectives which mean the opposite of the noun to which they are affixed.

10.4 *Verbs*

Once again we notice that there is fairly rich intracategorial verbal morphology while intercategorial relations with nouns, adjectives and adverbs are highly limited. Although the main burden of tense marking is carried by the auxiliary in MH, presence or absence of futurity is marked in the main verb; the main verb is also marked for person, gender, aspect and mood. Verbal strategies should also account for causatives and participles. Given these facts, it is not surprising that there are 59 WFSs that relate verbal forms among themselves. Most of these strategies involve either identity (WFSs 176-197) or suffixation (WFSs 198-223). The 22 WFSs involving identity underscore the fact, often overlooked, that the same verbal form serves a variety of functions. For example WFS 185 captures the fact that in the case of consonant ending verbs in MH, the *-a* ending past tense form remains invariant across changes of person. Strategies involving suffixation are largely concerned with the coding of the person, number, gender, tense and aspect distinctions into the verbal form. WFSs 203, 204, 211 and 224-231 are concerned with causatives; WFSs 207-209 with present and WFSs 198-200 and 202 with past participle; they are also concerned with imperfect and perfect aspect respectively; WFSs 232-234 with transitivity and WFS 210 with infinitives.

We have already briefly discussed the intercategorial relations obtaining between verbs on the one hand and adjectives and adverbs on the other. Since the WFSs are bidirectional, it does not make much sense in the framework used here to talk about denominal verbs and deverbal nouns. It has generally been suggested that it is more common to form verbs from nouns rather than nouns from verbs. In our description of MH morphology, there are 18 WFSs that relate nouns and verbs of which 13 involve simple suffixation (WFSs 102-114). Consider for example, the WFS:

107. $(X)_{\text{v, imper, nh}} \longleftrightarrow (Xai)_{\text{n, fem, sing}}$

which is located in the following set of words:

ləɽ	ləɽai
'fight'	'fight'
lɪkh	lɪkhai
'write'	'writing'
bʊn	bʊnai
'knit'	'knitting' etc.

In terms of computational complexity, nouns here (as in the case of all the other WFSs concerned with nouns and verbs) are more complex than the corresponding verbs; but these strategies allow the formation of *ləɽ* from *ləɽai* equally easily.

10.5 *Nouns*

A greater part of MH morphology is centred around nouns. Over 60% of the intra- and over 72% of the intercategorial WFSs are concerned with nouns. Again, intracategorially adjunction is the most favoured operation and suffixation and prefixation account for 72% of nominal strategies. Unlike other grammatical categories, nominal morphology also makes a fairly extensive use of the substitution operation (WFSs 87-99). Changes of case, number and gender are captured either through identity or suffixation or substitution but never through prefixation; suffixation, prefixation and substitution are all used to relate words with such semantic descriptors as 'dealer in X', 'related to X', 'doer of X' etc. with the corresponding, often morphologically simple, X. In fact, only one-third of the intracategorial nominal strategies are concerned with changes of case, number and gender; the remaining two-third capture ways of forming words with different dimensions of meaning.

10.6 *Morphophonemic Changes*

As will be clear from Tables 10.1, 10.2 and 10.3, morphophonemic change by itself or in combination with some other operation such as adjunction, substitution or deletion is rarely used in MH. There are only 3 WFSs which are based exclusively on morphophonemic changes; and there are only 25 WFSs in which morphophonemic change appears in combination with some other operation. Morphophonemic change is thus involved in about 10% of the WFSs of MH.

Morphophonemic change by itself is used in WFSs 232-234 to capture the transitivity relations obtaining among verbs. In these strategies, vowels are lengthened, lowered or nasalised to capture the relationship obtaining between intransitive and transitive verbs. Morphophonemic change is used most frequently in combination with suffixation, and once again more frequently intra- rather than intercategorially. It is interesting that there are 15 WFSs in MH in which in spite of two simultaneous operations viz. suffixation and morphophonemic change, the grammatical category does not change. This corresponds to the *crime-criminal* case, where in spite of *-məl* suffixation and *aɪ ~ ɪ* alternation both the words are nouns. WFSs 54-61 use morphophonemic change with suffixation in the case of nouns and WFSs 224-230 in the case of verbs. All these 15 WFSs are located intracategorially. For example, WFS 57 establishes the relationship between a set of masculine, singular nouns and the corresponding abstract nouns involving *-ai* suffixation with changes in vowel quality. Similarly, WFS 224 relates verbs with their corresponding Ist order causatives through simultaneous *-a* suffixation and morphophonemic change. Notice that these morphophonemic changes are tied to the sets of words in which they are located and are not across the board operations. The phonic changes involved are also of a minimal order being confined almost exclusively to. vowel lengthening and lowering.

Morphophohnemic change with suffixation is also used intercategorially, largely to relate nouns and verbs to the corresponding adjectives. Consider WFSs 155,156 and 166. All the three are concerned with nouns and adjectives; two involve *-ɪk* suffixation and the third i.e. WFS 166 *a~ɪk* substituiton. But the morphophonemic changes involved in each are different. That's why a simple WFS of the type:

$$(X)_{n} \longleftrightarrow (X\text{ɪ}k)_{adj}$$

won't do. The processes that relate *ərth-arthɪk* are quite different from the ones that relate *vɪdhan-vædhanɪk* on the one hand and *šɪkša-šaikšɪk* on the other. Hence we need three different WFSs.

Morphophonemic changes also appear a couple of times with deletion and substitution but never with prefixation. Prefixation stands distinguished from other morphological operations in that it is not accompanied by morphophonemic changes in MH.

10.7 *Minimization of Morphological Marks*

What might be called the non-unique nature of morphological marks is most clearly demonstrated by the fact that the same word-part is used for a large number of morphological purposes. Consider, for example, the word-part *-a* in our description of MH morphology. It participates in 30 WFSs involving identity, adjunction, substitution and deletion. It can perform the following functions in MH:

(1) Change gender of nouns (e.g. WFS 14);
(2) Participate in substitution strategies to change number and case (e.g. WFS 89);
(3) Participate in a deletion strategy to obtain intercategorial relations between verbs and nouns (e.g. WFS 115);
(4) Turn nouns into adjectives (e.g. WFS 127);
(5) Participate in a substitution strategy to establish a relationship between nouns and adverbs (e.g. WFS 175);

(6) Participate in identity relationships to neutralise distinctions of person in the verb (e.g. WFS 185);
(7) Make Ist order causatives through suffixation (e.g. WFS 203);
(8) Mark person distinctions in the verb (e.g. WFS 202);
(9) Make adjectives from verbs through suffixation (e.g. WFS 237);
(10) Participate in substitution strategies to mark gender distinctions in adjectives (e.g. WFS 263);
(11) Participate in substitution strategies to establish relationship between adjectives and adverbs (e.g. WFS 270);
(12) Make perfect participle through suffixation (e.g. WFS 202).

The word-part *-a,* in other words, knows no boundaries either of grammatical categories or grammatical features. It also cuts across the traditional 'inflections vs. derivation' distinction; it can not only change number, case and gender but also form adjectives from verbs and adverbs.

On the other hand, we notice a trend towards maximizing morphological marks underscoring again, though in a different way, the non-unique nature of morphology. It is clear from the description in Chapter 8 that several formal marks will often be used to achieve the same ends. Thus nominal plurals in Hindi may involve identity (e.g. WFSs 3-7), *-ẽ* (WFS 13), *-o* (WFS 15), *-õ* (WFS 17) *-at* (WFS 24), *-an* (WFS 25), *-yã* (WFS 29), *-yõ* (WFS 30) and *-yo* (WFS 31) suffixation and *a-e* (WFS 88), *a-u* (WFS 92) and *a-õ* (WFS 90) substitution.

10.8 *Non-Morphemic Morphemes*

We have already discussed in some detail the case of *nominate-nominee* in Chapter 4. We argued against positing abstract forms such as *nomin* as morphemes since they do not have any recognizable status for the speaker. Our description in Chapter 8 provides several examples of what one may wish to call non-morphemic morphemes. These demonstrate that the results of formal analytical capacities may not always correspond to certain semantic articulations. We have used the variables P, Q, R etc (rather than X) to denote such word-parts. WFSs 88-99 involving substitution are good examples of this phenomenon. For example, WFS 91 establishes a relationship between *-a* ending nominative singular masculine nouns and the corresponding *-e* ending oblique singular/vocative singular/nominative plural forms, being located in pairs of words, e.g. *ləɽka* ~ *ləɽke; ghoɽa* ~ *ghoɽe; məkbəra* ~ *məkbəre* etc . where **ləɽk, *ghoɽ* and **məkbər* are not words; they are only word-parts. It will of course be possible for a speaker of Hindi to come across a new word that fits the LHS of the WFS in question, analyze the word and, produce a new word corresponding to the RHS of that WFS or the other way round.

10.9 *Hindi Causatives*

We need several strategies to account for causative formation in MH. These WFSs may involve identity or suffixation with or without morphophonemic change or substitution. Though *-a* (WFS 203) and *-va* (WFS 211) suffixation are the two most frequently used strategies to produce Ist and IInd order causatives, they often produce forms that are semantically only derived transitives. In the case of verbs which are already transitive e.g. *sɪl* 'stitch', *-a* and *-va* suffixation produces forms that are identical in meaning. In the case of reflexive verbs e.g. *pi* 'drink', *-a* suffixation only produces a derived transitive rather than a true causative. It is only in the case of real activity verbs e.g. *gɪr* 'fall', that the application of WFSs 203 and 211 produces true Ist and IInd order causatives in *gɪra* and *gɪrva*. Causatives are related to their corresponding verbal forms through identity (WFSs 177, 178 and 180), suffixation (WFSs 203, 204 and 224-236) and substitution (WFS 231). Notice that of the nine suffixation WFSs, 4 involve *-a* suffixation. These cannot be collapsed into one because they cover different sets of words. For example, the *-a* suffixation in WFS 224 involves a morphophonemic change that changes vowel length; in WFS 226, *-a* adjunction is accompanied by a morphophonemic change that also involves vowel height. Again, both WFS 225 and 228 involve *-va* suffixation but each is accompanied by different morphophonemic changes. WFSs 227, 229 and 230 pertain to that set of verbal pairs where causatives are formed by *-la* and *-lva* suffixation with some morphophonemic changes. Most verbs which have IInd order causatives in *-va* or *-lva* suffixation have first order causatives in *-a* and *-la*. However, there is a small set of verbs sharing the structure (Pol) e.g. *bol* 'speak', *khol* 'open', *ghol* 'mix' which form causatives only with *-va*. Finally, there is a small category of verbs e.g. *ja*, 'go', *a* 'come' etc. which do not enter into causative morphology at all.

10.10 *Multiple Affixation*

Considerable attention has been paid to the distinction between non-neutral ('primary' or 'weak boundary') and 'secondary' affixes and the sequential order of morphemes in a word (e.g. Bloomfield 1933; Chomsky and Halle 1968). Since stress is largely non-phonemic in Hindi, the question

of stress-attracting non-neutral primary affixes looks irrelevant. WFSs arise out of the sets of words in which they are located and it is these sets which define the order of word-parts in a given complex word. All the routes of arriving at a morphologically complex word remain open.
Consider the following set of words

ləjja	nɪrləjj
'shame'	'shameless'
dəya	nɪrdəy
'kindness'	'heartless'

In most morphological descriptions, abstract 'roots' of the form *ləjj* and *dəy* will be posited and then *-a* suffixation will generate nouns e.g. *ləjja* and *dəya* and *nɪr-* prefixation adjectives e.g. *nɪrləjj* and *nɪrdəy*. In the theory adopted in this book, entities like *ləjj* have no ontological status. What exists is the set of words involving simultaneous deletion and prefixation leading to a WFS of the type

$(\text{Pa})_{n} \longleftrightarrow (\text{nɪrP})_{adj}$

Suppose one wishes to arrive at a fairly complex Hindi word *əntərraštriyta* 'internationalism', the number of ways open to one are really large e.g.

raštr	⟷	əntərraštrɪy
'nation' (noun)		'international' (adj)
raštrɪy	⟷	raštrɪyta
'national' (adj)		'nationalism' (noun)

Notice that getting to nouns from nouns through adjectives is only one way of doing so. Nothing stops one from getting to the noun-2 or noun-3 directly. What is not allowed in Hindi is *əntəraštr* or *raštrta* or *əntərraštrta*. *-ta* suffixation demands an adjective as input; *əntər-* can be prefixed either to adjectives or nouns (*-ta* ending in this case).

10.11 *Dormant Strategies*

In 8.11 we have listed some of the dormant strategies of Hindi word-formation. We could find only one pair of words as an example for each of these relationships. Notice that most of these strategies involve morphophonemic changes with or without suffixation. In fact, there are several examples of the well known *'crime-criminal'* case where the grammatical category remains unchanged in spite of two morphological operations: suffixation and morphophonemic change. Consider DS 10:

$(\text{khaj})_{\text{n, fem, sing}} \longleftrightarrow (\text{khʊjli})_{\text{n, fem, sing}}$
'itch' 'itchiness'

Here *-li* is suffixed and *a* changes to *ʊ*. Both these markers do not form a part of our description of Hindi WFSs. *-li* is not a noun-forming affix, nor do we notice a~ʊ alternation in any of the WFSs. These two words are obviously related and relatable but are simply listed without any analysis of the relationship involved. Until we get another pair like *khaj ~ khʊjli*, we cannot talk in terms of an active WFS.

10.12 MH *Morphology and Morphology in General*

Although the picture presented above confirms the generally held views that morphology is typically concatenative and that morphophonology is only sparingly used as an exclusive marker of morphological category or function (cf. Dressler and Barbarcsi 1994: 41-42), it is important to underline the facts that non-concatenative morphology does show up in languages such as MH and that morphophonology does in fact function as full-blooded morphology. Both facts should oblige us to re-examine the neo-Pāṇinian devices by which non-concatenative morphology was assimilated to concatenative morphology and morphophonology to phonology. The most important of these devices have been the morphological zero and the construct 'root'. Our description makes it clear that these devices are not only not needed but also that they create descriptive as well as explanatory problems. Once the morphological role of morphophonology and of identity, obviously limited because of the sorts of factors Dressler (1985, 1992, and forthcoming) draws our attention to, is clearly recognized, the morphological zero becomes entirely dispensible. It is worth reminding the reader that identity is exploited by MH much more than its relatively free word order could lead one to suspect. And the recognition of substitution as a valid morphological operation allows us to dispense with the un-necessarily abstract unit called 'root'.

There are, of course, MH-particular facts that appear to be unrelated to any general principles or issues. The reversal of morphological richness between MH Verbs and Adjectives along the intra-/intercategorial dimension, for example, must remain a datum for a yet-to-be-developed theory of morphological typology (cf. Sapir 1921). We also cannot say precisely what the richness (both intra- and inter-categorial) of MH nominal morphology is related to (either within MH or typologically). Facts of this sort, we would like to suggest, can be made sense of only when full morphological descriptions of other languages become available. At the moment, the pre-occupation with what some of us like to call 'linguistic theory' keeps us away from undertaking such detailed descriptions. We hope this description of MH would be seen as an invitation to undertake similar descriptions of other languages. When that is done, we should be able not only to raise some further morphological questions but also answer them.

APPENDIX I

Word Formation Strategies: A Summary

W.F.S. No.	Grammatical categories involved	Word-part involved	Feature changes	Morphological Operation
1	n	ø	nom - obl	identity
2	n	ø	nom - voc	identity
3	n	ø	sing - pl	identity
4	n	ø	obl, sing - nom, pl	identity
5	n	ø	voc, sing - nom, pl	identity
6	n	ø	obl,sing - nom, pl	identity
7	n	ø	voc, sing - nom, pl	identity
8	n	-i	one who deals in X	suffixation
9	n	-i	one who practices X	suffixation
10	n	-i	hailing from X	suffixation
11	n	-e	abs X	suffixation
12	n	-i	masc, fem	suffixation
13	n	-ẽ	sing - pl, nom	suffixation
14	n	-a	masc - fem	suffixation
15	n	-o	sing - voc, pl	suffixation
16	n	-o	nom - voc	suffixation
17	n	-õ	sing - obl, pl	suffixation
18	n	-õ	nom - obl, pl	suffixation
19	n	-oi	X's husband	suffixation
20	n	-ɪk	user of X	suffixation
21	n	-ɪn	masc - fem	suffixation
22	n	-ək	doer of X	suffixation
23	n	-ək	ono - abs X	suffixation
24	n	-at	sing - pl	suffixation
25	n	-an	sing - pl	suffixation
26	n	-ci	user of X	suffixation
27	n	-ni	masc - fem	suffixation
28	n	-ṛa	dimi X	suffixation

29	n	-yã	sing - nom, pl	suffixation
30	n	-yõ	nom - obl (fem)	suffixation
31	n	-yo	nom - voc	suffixation
32	n	-ɪya	dealer in X	suffixation
33	n	-ɪye	dealer(s) in X	suffixation
34	n	-ɪyõ	dealers in X	suffixation
35	n	-ɪyo	dealers in X	suffixation
36	n	-ɪzm	abs X izm	suffixation
37	n	-ani	masc - fem	suffixation
38	n	-ana	related to X	suffixation
39	n	-kar	creator of X	suffixation
40	n	-kar	abs X	suffixation
41	n	-gər	doer of X	suffixation
42	n	-dan	container for X	suffixation
43	n	-dar	having X	suffixation
44	n	-pən	state of being X	suffixation
45	n	-baz	skilled user of X	suffixation
46	n	-saz	maker of X	suffixation
47	n	-xor	indulging in X	suffixation
48	n	-van	possessor of X	suffixation
49	n	-iyət	abs X	suffixation
50	n	-aləy	place of X	suffixation
51	n	-gɪrɪ	what X does	suffixation
52	n	-nama	document of X	suffixation
53	n	-vala	dealing in X	suffixation
54	n	-r	one who deals in X	suffixation with MC
55	n	-æt	practising X	suffixation with MC
56	n	-ɪn	masc - fem	suffixation with MC
57	n	-ai	abs X	suffixation with MC
58	n	-ari	related to X	suffixation with MC
59	n	-ɪyo	dimi of X	suffixation with MC
60	n	-ɪya	dimi of X	suffixiaton with MC
61	n	-ola	dimi of X	suffixation with MC
62	n	ə-	opposite of X	prefixation
63	n	əv-	specific X	prefixation
64	n	up-	smaller than X	prefixation
65	n	ʊd-	related to X	prefixation
66	n	kʊ-	bad X	prefixation
67	n	be-	Xlessness	prefixation

68	n	be-	person without X	prefixation
69	n	na-	not X	prefixation
70	n	sə-	good X	prefixation
71	n	sʊ-	good X	prefixation
72	n	vɪ-	opposite of X	prefixation
73	n	vɪ-	intensified X	prefixation
74	n	ədhɪ-	special X	prefixation
75	n	əbhɪ-	excess of X	prefixation
76	n	ənʊ-	involving X	prefixation.
77	n	pəɽ-	great/other X	prefixation
78	n	prə-	intensified X	prefixation
79	n	dʊr-	bad X	prefixation
80	n	sər-	head of X	prefixation
81	n	səh-	co-X	prefixation
82	n	həm-	person with the same X as the speaker	prefixation
83	n	svə-	own X	prefixation
84	n	pəri -	intensified X	prefixation
85	n	prətɪ-	every X	prefixation
86	n	prətɪ-	counter X	prefixation
87	n	a - i	masc - fem	substitution
88	n	a - e	nom sing - obl/sing/ voc/sing/nom pl	substitution
89	n	a - o	nom sing - voc pl	substitution
90	n	a - õ	nom sing - obl pl	substitution
91	n	a - ək	doer of X	substitution
92	n	a - u	endeared X	substitution
93	n	a - e	address	substitution
94	n	i - a	big X	substitution
95	n	i - ɪyã	nom pl	substitution
96	n	i - ɪyõ	obl pl	substitution
97	n	i - ɪyo	voc pl	substitution
98	n	ək - ɪka	masc-fem	substitution
99	n	na - ək	doer of X	substitution
100	n,v	ø	v - n	identity
101	n,v	ø	v - n	identity
102	n,v	-ẽ	v - n	suffixation
103	n,v	-o	v - n	suffixation
104	n,v	-õ	v - n	suffixation

105	n,v	-ək	v - n	suffixation
106	n,v	-ən	v - n	suffixation
107	n,v	-ai	v - n	suffixation
108	n,v	-an	v - n	suffixation
109	n,v	-av	v - n	suffixation
110	n,v	-ni	v - n	suffixation
111	n,v	-na	v - n	suffixation
112	n,v	-va	v - n	suffixation
113	n,v	-vəṭ	v - n	suffixation
114	n,v	-həṭ	v - n	suffixation
115	n,v	a - ø	v - n	deletion
116	n,v	a - ø	v - n	deletion with MC
117	n,v	ɪya - ø	v- n	deletion with MC
118	n, adj	(i)	n - adj	identity
119	n, adj	(baz)	n - adj	identity
120	n, adj	(vər)	n - adj	identity
121	n, adj	(var)	n - adj	identity
122	n, adj	(van)	n - adj	identity
123	n, adj	(mənd)	n - adj	identity
124	n, adj	(əsvi)	n - adj	identity
125	n, adj	(əndaz)	n - adj	identity
126	n, adj	-i	n - adj	suffixation
127	n, adj	-a	n - adj	suffixation
128	n, adj	-ɪt	n - adj	suffixation
129	n, adj	-in	n - adj	suffixation
130	n, adj	-ɪl	n - adj	suffixation
131	n, adj	-dã	n - adj	suffixation
132	n, adj	-lʊ	n - adj	suffixation
133	n, adj	-ɪya	n - adj	suffixation
134	n, adj	-ida	n - adj	suffixation
135	n, adj	-ila	n - adj	suffixation
136	n, adj	-ani	n - adj	suffixation
137	n, adj	-ana	n - adj	suffixation
138	n, adj	-gar	n - adj	suffixation
139	n, adj	-dar	n - adj	suffixation
140	n, adj	-baz	n - adj	suffixation
141	n, adj	-nak	n - adj	suffixation
142	n, adj	-niy	n - adj	suffixation
143	n, adj	-məy	n - adj	suffixation

144	n, adj	-xez	n - adj	suffixation
145	n, adj	-van	n - adj	suffixation
146	n, adj	-vər	n - adj	suffixation
147	n, adj	-var	n - adj	suffixation
148	n, adj	-sar	n - adj	suffixation
149	n, adj	-əsvi	n - adj	suffixation
150	n, adj	-nʊma	n - adj	suffixation
151	n, adj	-mənd	n - adj	suffixation
152	n, adj	-šʊda	n - adj	suffixation
153	n, adj	-vənt	n - adj	suffixation
154	n, adj	-əndaz	n - adj	suffixation
155	n, adj	-ɪk	n - adj	suffixation with MC
156	n, adj	-ɪk	n - adj	suffixation with MC
157	n, adj	-æl	n - adj	suffixation with MC
158	n, adj	ə-	opposite of X	prefixation
159	n, adj	nɪ-	neg X	prefixation
160	n, adj	la-	neg X	prefixation
161	n, adj	həm-	with X	prefixation
162	n, adj	nɪr-	Xless	prefixation
163	n, adj	nɪš-	Xless	prefixation
164	n, adj	ɛ-cdar	n - adj	substitution
165	n, adj	na-niy	n - adj	substitution with MC
166	n, adj	a-ɪk	n - adj	substitution with MC
167	n, adj	a-era	n - adj	substitution with MC
168	n, adv	-ən	n - adv	suffixation
169	n, adv	-ak	n - adv	suffixation
170	n, adv	-var	n - adv	suffixation
171	n, adv	bə-	n - adv	prefixation
172	n, adv	ba-	n - adv	prefixation
173	n, adv	be-	n - adv	prefixation
174	n, adv	sə-	n - adv	prefixation
175	n, adv	a-e	n - adv	substitution
176	v	ø	masc - fem	identity
177	v	ø	Ist caus	identity
178	v	ø	IInd caus	identity
179	v	(i)	I-IInh/III	identity
180	v	(ĩ)	I-II/III	identity
181	v	(e)	I-II / III	identity
182	v	(ẽ)	IInh - III	identity

183	v	(e)	pl - sing IInh/III	identity
184	v	(ẽ)	l - III	identity
185	v	(a)	I - IInh / III	identity
186	v	(a)	intr - tr / Ist caus	identity
187	v	(na)	nh - h	identity
188	v	(ya)	I - IInh	identity
189	v	(tĩ)	I - IInh	identity
190	v	(te)	I - II/III	identity
191	v	(ta)	I - IInh / III	identity
192	v	(ti)	I - II / III	identity
193	v	(ɪye)	sing - pl	identity
194	v	(egi)	III - IInh	identity
195	v	(ẽgi)	I - IInh / III	identity
196	v	(ega)	III - IInh	identity
197	v	(ɪyega)	sing - pl	identity
198	v	-i	I/IInh/ III	suffixation
199	v	-ĩ	I/II/III	suffixation
200	v	-e	I/II/III	suffixation
201	v	-e	I/II h / III	suffixation
202	v	-a	I/ IInh / III	suffixation
203	v	-a	Ist caus /tra	suffixation
204	v	-a	IInd caus	suffixation
205	v	-ũ	I, sing	suffixation
206	v	-o	II	suffixation
207	v	-ti	pres p	suffixation
208	v	-te	pres p	suffixation
209	v	-ta	pres p	suffixation
210	v	-na	inf	suffixation
211	v	-va	IInd caus	suffixation
212	v	-ya	I/ IInh/ III	suffixation
213	v	-ye	I/ IInh/ III	suffixation
214	v	-ɪye	IIh	suffixation
215	v	-egi	IInh /III	suffixation
216	v	-ẽgi	I/ IInh/ III	suffixation
217	v	-ega	IInh/ III	suffixation
218	v	-ẽge	I/ III	suffixation
219	v	-ogi	II	suffixation
220	v	-oge	II	suffixation
221	v	-ũgi	I	suffixation

222	v	-ũga	I	suffixation
223	v	-ɪyega	IIh	suffixation
224	v	-a	Ist caus	suffixation with MC
225	v	-a	IInd caus	suffixation with MC
226	v	-a	Ist caus	suffixation with MC
227	v	-la	Ist caus	suffixation with MC
228	v	- va	IInd caus	suffixation with MC
229	v	-lva	IInd caus	suffixation with MC
230	v	-lva	IInd caus	suffixation with MC
231	v	a-va	IInd caus	substitution
232	v	v change	intr - tr	MC
233	v	v change	intr - tr	MC
234	v	v change	intr - tr	MC
235	v, adj	-i	v - adj	suffixation
236	v, adj	-e	v - adj	suffixation
237	v, adj	-a	v - adj	suffixation
238	v, adj	-u	v - adj	suffixation
239	v, adj	-au	v - adj	suffixation
240	v, adj	-ti	v - adj	suffixation
241	v, adj	-te	v - adj	suffixation
242	v, adj	-ta	v - adj	suffixation
243	v, adj	-vĩ	v - adj	suffixation
244	v, adj	-vã	v - adj	suffixation
245	v, adj	-ya	v - adj	suffixation
246	v, adj	-ila	v - adj	suffixation
247	v, adj	-ɪya	v - adj	suffixation
248	v, adj	-ɪyəl	v - adj	suffixation
249	v, adj	-vəni	v - adj	suffixation with MC
250	v, adj	-ya	v - adj	suffixation with MC
251	v, adj	-əkkeɽ	v - adj	suffixation with MC
252	v, adj	u-ʊa	v - adj	substitution
253	v, adj	u-ʊi	v - adj	substitution
254	v, adv	-e	v - adv	suffixation
255	v, adv	-ti	v - adv	suffixation
256	v, adv	-te	v - adv	suffixation
257	v, adv	-ta	v - adv	suffixation
258	v, adv	-kər	v - adv	suffixation
259	adj	-ø	masc - fem	identity
260	adj	-tər	comp.	suffixation

261	adj	-təm	super	suffixation
262	adj	məha	inten X	prefixation
263	adj	a - i	masc-fem	substitution
264	adj	a - e	sing-pl	substitution
265	adj	vi - vni	masc-fem	substitution with MC
266	adj, adv	-ən	adj-adv	suffixation
267	adj, adv	-tər	adj-adv	suffixation
268	adj, adv	-kər	adj-adv	suffixation
269	adj, adv	-təya	adj-adv	suffixation
270	adj, adv	a - e	adj-adv	substitution

Appendix II

Specified Material in Hindi WFSs

(Listed largely according to the Hindi alphabet within each category: ə, a, ɪ, i, ʊ, u, e, æ, o, ɔ, k, c, ṭ, t, p series; y, r, l, v, s, š, h; nasalised vowels precede oral vowels)

Identity
1-7, 100, 101, 118-125, 176-197, 258

Suffixation
(Strategies involving morphophonemic change are starred *)

-ək 22, 23, 105
-əkkəṛ 251
-ən 106, 168, 265
-əndaz 154
-əsvi 149
-a 14, 127, 202-204, 224*, 226*, 237
-ai 57*, 107
-au 239
-ak 169
-at 24
-an 25, 108
-ana 38, 137
-ani 37, 136
-ari 58*
-av 109
-ɪk 155*, 156*, 166*
-ɪt 128
-ɪn 56*
-ɪyəl 248
-ɪya 32, 59*, 60*, 133, 247
-ɪye 33, 214
-ɪyega 223
-ɪyõ 34
-ɪyo 35

-dar 43, 139
-na 111, 210
-nak 141
-nama 52
-ni 27, 110
-niy 142
-nʊma 150
-pən 44
-baz 45, 140
-məy 143
-mənd 151
-yã 29
-ya 212, 245
-yõ 30
-yo 31
-r 54*
-la 227*
-lu 132
-lva 229*, 230*
-vəni 249
-vənt 153
-vəʈ 113
-vər 146
-vã 244
-va 112, 211, 225*, 228*
-van 48, 145
-var 147, 170
-vala 53
-vĩ 243
-sar 148
-saz 46
-šʊda 152
-həʈ 114
-xor 47
-xez 144
-ɽa 28

Prefixation

Substitution

a~era 167*
a~edar 164
a~õ 90
a-o 89
a-u 92
a-va 231
i-ɪyã 95
i-ɪyõ 96
i-ɪyo 97
u-ʊa 252
u-ʊi 253
na - ək 99
na~nɪy 165
vi - vɪni 264

Deletion

-a 115, 116*
-ɪya 117*

Morphophonemic change
V ~ V 232

V	~	V233
+high		- high
-long		+long

V ~ V 234

APPENDIX III

MAJOR MORPHOLOGICAL PROCESSES

A. Intracategorial

Nouns

1. Numbers changes
   (a) Identity
       WFS3
   (b) Suffixation
       WFSs 24,25
2. Case changes
   (a) Indentity
       WFSs 1,2
   (b) Suffixation
       WFSs 16,18,31
3. Gender changes
   (a) Suffixation
       WFSs 12,14,19,21,27,37
   (b) Suffixation with morphophonemic change
       WFS 56
4. Abstract nouns
   (a) Suffixation
       WFSs 11,23,36,40,49
   (b) Suffixation with morphophonemic changes
       WFS 57
5. Agentives : dealing in, doing, making or practising X
   (a) Suffixation
       WFSs 8,9,22,32,33,34,35,41,46,53,54,55
   (b) Substitution
       WFS 99
6. Antonyms : bad X or oppsite of X
   (a) Prefixation
       WFSs 62,66,69,72,79
7. User of X
   (a) Suffixation
       WFSs 20,26,45,47

8. Diminutives
    (a) Suffixation with morphophonemic changes
        WFSs 59,60,61
9. Good, great or intensified X
    (a) Prefixation
        WFSs 70,71,73,77,78,84
10. Case and number changes
    (a) Indentity
        WFSs 4,5,6,7
    (b) Suffixation
        WFSs 13,15,17,29
    (c) Substitution
        WFSs 88,89,90,95,96,97

Verbs

1. Person
    (a) Indentity
        WFSs 179,180,181,182,184,185,188,189,190, 191,194,195,196
    (b) Suffixation
        WFSs 98,199,200,201,202,206,212,213,215, 216,217,218,219,220,221,222
2. Number
    (a) Indentity
        WFSs 183,193,197
    (b) Suffixation
        WFS 205
3. Gender
    (a) Indentity
        WFS 176
4. Aspect and participles
    (a) Suffixation
        WFSs 202,207,208,209,212,213
5. Causatives
    (a) Indentity
        WFSs 177,178,186
    (b) Suffixation
        WFSs 203,204,211

(c) Suffixation with morphophonemic change
WFSs 224,225,226,227,228,229,230
(d) Substitution
WFS 231
6. Transitivity
(a) Indentity
WFS 186
(b) Suffixation
WFS 203
(c) Morphophonemic change
WFSs 232,233,234
7. Honorificity
(a) Indentity
WFS 187
(b) Suffixation
WFSs 201,214,223

Adjectives

1. Comparative
(a) Suffixation
WFS 260
2. Superlative
(a) Suffixation
WFS 261
3. Gender
(a) Indentity
WFS 259
(b) Substitution
WFSs 263,265
4. Number
(a) Substitution
WFS 264

B. Intercategorial

1. Nouns–Verbs
(a) Indentity
WFSs 100,101
(b) Suffixation
WFSs 102–114

(c) Deletion
WFS 115
(d) Deletion with morphophonemic change
WFSs 116,117

2. Nouns–Adjectives
(a) Indentity
WFSs 118–125
(b) Suffixation
WFSs 126–154
(c) Suffixation with morphophonemic change
WFSs 155–157
(d) Prefixation
WFSs 158–163
(e) Substitution
WFS 164
(f) Substitution with morphophonemic change
WFSs 165–167

3. Nouns–Adverbs
(a) Suffixation
WFSs 168–170
(b) Prefixation
WFSs 171–174
(c) Substitution
WFS 175

4. Verbs–Adjectives
(a) Suffixation
WFSs 235–238
(b) Suffixation with morphophonemic change
WFSs 249–251
(c) Substitution
WFSs 252,253

5. Verbs–Adverbs
(a) Suffixation
WFSs 254–258

6. Adjectives–Adverbs
(a) Suffixation
WFSs 266–269
(b) Substitution
WFS 270

BIBLIOGRAPHY

Abbi, A. 1980. *Semantic Grammar of Hindi: A Study in Reduplication.* New Delhi: Bahri Publications.

Allen, W.S. 1962. *Sandhi.* The Hague: Mouton.

Anderson, S. 1982. Where's Morphology. *Linguistic Inquiry* 13:571-612.

Aronoff, M. 1976. *Word Formation in Generative Grammar.* Cambridge, Mass.: MIT Press.

Aronoff, M. and Sridhar, S.N. 1983. Morphological levels in English and Kannada; or Atarizing Reagan. In Richardson, J. et al, eds. *Papers from Parasession on the Interplay of Phonology, Morphology and Syntax.* Chicago: Chicago Linguistic Society, 3-16.

Austin, J.L. 1956. A plea for Excuses. In Chappell, V.C., ed.,1964 *Ordinary Language, Contempopary Perspective in Phillosophy Series.* Prentice Hall, 41-63.

Bahri, U. S. 1981. ed. *Topics in Hindi Linguistics,* Vol. 1. New Delhi: Bahri Publications.

Baker, M. 1985. The Mirror Principle and Morphosyntactic Example. *Language* 16: 373-415.

Bauer, L. 1985. *English Word Formation.* Cambridge: Cambridge University Press.

Beams, J. 1872. *A Comparative Grammar of the Modern Aryan Languages of India.* London: Trubner & Co.

Beligatti, C.1761. *Alphabetum Brammhanicum.* Kasi: Romae.

Benson, J. W.1990. *Patanjali's Remarks on Aṅga.* Oxford: Oxford University Press.

Bever, T. G. Carroll, J. and Hurtig, R. 1976. Analogy. In Bever, T. G. Katz, J. J. and Langendoen, T. D. eds. *An Integrated Theory of Linguistic Ability.* New York: Thoms Crott Press.

Bharati, S.1988. *Some Aspects of Phonology of Hindi and English.* CIEFL, Hyderabad, Ph.D Thesis.

Bhatia T. K. 1987. *A History of the Hindi Grammatical Tradition: Hindi-Hindustani Grammar, Grammarians, History and Problems.* Leiden: E.J. Brill.

Bloomfield, L. 1933. *Language*. New York: Holt, Rinehart & Winston.

Burton-Page, J. 1957. The Syntax of Participial Forms in Hindi. *BSOAS* 19.1:94-104.

Bybee, J. 1980. Morphophonemic Change from Inside and Outside the Paradigm. *Lingua* 50:45-59.

Cardona, G. 1974. *Panini : A Survey of Research*. Delhi: Motilal Banarsidass

Carrier, J. 1975. Reduplication in Tagalog. Unpublished Manuscript. Cambridge: Mass.

Carroll, J. 1974. Linguistic Performance and Diachronic Analogy. Paper read at the LSA Meeting Amherst.

Chêne, B. 1975. The Treatment of Analogy in a Formal Grammar. In de Grossman, R. E., San, L. J., and Vance, T.J. eds. *Papers from the 11th CLS Meeting*. Chicago: Chicago Linguistic Society.

Chomsky, N. 1970. Remarks on Nominalization. In Jacobs, R. and Rosenbaum, P. eds. *Readings in English Transformational Grammar*. Waltham, Mass.: Basil Blackwell.

Chomsky, N. and Halle, M. 1968. *The Sound Pattern of English*. New York: Harper & Row Publishers.

Darden, W. 1974. *Introduction to the CLS Parasession on Natural Phonology*. Chicago: Chicago Linguistic Society.

de Bleser, R. and Bayer, J. 1988. On the Role of Inflectional Morphology in Agrammatism. In Hammond, M. and Noonan M., eds. 45-70.

Desrochers, R. 1990. *La the'orie de la Marque*. Montreal, Ph.D.Thesis.

Di Sciullo, A.M. and Williams, E.1987. *On the Definition of Word* Cambridge: Mass.: MIT Press.

Dressler, W.U. 1985. *Morphophonology: The Dynamics of Derivation*. Ann Arbor: Carona Press.

_______. 1996. A Functionalist Semiotic Model of Morphology. In Singh, R. ed. *Trubetzkoy's Orphan*. Amsterdam: John Benjamin.

Dressler, W.U. and Barbaresi. L. M. 1994. *Morphopragmatics*. Berlin.

D'Souza, J. 1985. Schwa Syncope and Vowel Nasalization in Hindi-Urdu: A Non-linear Approach. *Studies in the Linguistic Sciences* 15.1:11-30.

Dua, H. 1969. *The Verbal Piece in Spoken Hindi: A Morphosyntactic Study*. York, U.K, Ph.D. Thesis.

Elizarenkova, T. Y. 1988. Morphophonology of Hindi. In Andronov, M.S. and Mallik, B. P. eds. *Linguistics : A Soviet Approach*. (*Indian Journal of Lingustics*) Calcutta, :367-386.

Ethrington, W. 1871. *Bhasha-Bhaskar, Arthat Hindi Bhasha Ka Vyakarna*. Lahore: Indian House.

Fanselow, G.1988. Word-Syntax and Semantic Principles. In Booij,G. and Marle J.V. eds. *Yearbook of Morphology.* Dordrecht: Foris.

Farkas, D., Jacobson, W. M. and Todrys, K.W. eds. 1978. *CLS Papers from the Parasession on the Lexicon.* Chicago: Chicago Linguistic Society.

Ford, A. 1982. La Place de la Morphophonologie dans la Grammaire. Revue de l' associoations Quebeçoise de Linguistique. 2.2:73-80.

Ford, A. and Singh, R. 1983. On the Status of Morphophonology. In Richardson, J. et al, eds. *The Interplay of Phonology, Morphology and Syntax.* Chicago: Chicago Linguistic Society.

________. 1984. Remarks on the Directionality of Word-formation Processes. In Alvarez, G. et al. eds. *ESCOL 1984.* Columbus: Ohio State University Press, 205-213.

________. 1985. Towards a Non-paradigmatic Morphology. In Niepokuy, M. et al. eds. Proceedings of the 11th Annual Meeting of the Berkeley Linguistic Society, *BLS 11*:87-95

_______. 1991. Propedeutique Morphologique. *Folia Linguistica* 25.3 & 4:549-75.

Ford, A., Singh, R. and Martoharadjono, G. In Press. *Pace Pāṇini: Towards a Word-based Theory of Morphology.* New York:Peter Lang

Gilchrist, J.B.1796. *A Grammar of the Hindoostani Language.* Calcutta: The Chronicle Press. Rpt. Menston: The Scolar Press, 1970.

Gumperz, J.J. and Naim, C.M. 1971. Formal and Informal Standards in the Hindi Regional Language Area. In Dil, A. S. ed. *Language in Social Groups.* Stanford: Stanford University Press, 48-76.

Gupta, K. 1972. *Hindi Upsargõ kaa Bhaashaa Vaigyaanik Adhyayan.* Delhi, M.A. Dissertation.

Guru, K.P. 1920. *Hindi Vyakaran.* Kashi: Lakshami Narayan Press. (1962 edition).

Hackman, G.J. 1976. *An Integrated Analysis of the Hindi Tense and Aspect System.* Illinois, Ph.D. thesis.

Hadley, G. 1772. Grammatical Remarks on the Practical and Vulgar Dialet of Indostan Language. Menston : The Scolar Press (For details see Bhatia 1987).

Halle, M. 1973. Prolegomena to a Theory of Word Formation. *Linguistic Inquiry* 4:3-16.

Hammond, M. and Noonan, M. eds. 1988. *Theoretical Morphology: Approaches in Modern Linguistics.* San Diego: Academic Press.

Hjemslev, L. 1963. *Prolegomena to a Theory of Language.* Tr from the Danish, 1943 by Francis J. Whitfield. Bloomington: Indiana University Press.

Hockett, C.F. 1958. *A Course in Modern Linguistics.* New York: Macmillan.

Householder, F.W. 1966. Phonological Theory: A Brief Comment. *Journal of Linguistics,* 2:99-100.

Jackendoff, R. 1975. Morphological and Semantic Regularities in the Lexicon. *Language* 51:63-71.

Jain, M.S. 1976. *Hindi me Ruupagrammik Vishleshan kii kuch sammasyaaẽ.* Jabalpur.

Kachru, Y. 1966. *An Introduction to Hindi Syntax.* Urbana: Department of Linguistics.

______ 1980. *Aspects of Hindi Grammar.* New Delhi: Manohar Publications.

Kelkar, A. 1968. *Studies in Hindi-Urdu I : Introduction and Word Phonology.* Poona: Deccan College.

Kellogg, S.H. 1876. (3rd ed. 1938) *A Grammar of the Hindi Language.* London: Routledge and Kegan Paul.

Ketelaar, J.T. 1698. *Instruction or Teaching of the Hindustani and Persian Languages.* MS. (for details of the title, authorship, dates of publication etc., see Bhatia 1987:21-23)

Khubchandani, L.M. 1978. Towards a Selection Grammar: Fluidity in Modes of Address and Reference in Hindi-Urdu. *Indian Linguistics* 39. 1-4:1-24.

Kiparsky, P. 1982a. Lexical Morphology and Phonology. In Yange, I. S.ed. *Linguistics in the Morning Calm.* Seoul: Hanshin Publishers.

______1982b From Cyclic Phonology to Lexical Phonology. In van der Hulst, and Smith, N. eds. *The Structure of Phonological Representations.* Dordrecht: Foris, 131-175.

______1985 Some Consequences of Lexical Phonology. In Ewen, C. and Anderson, J. eds. *Phonology Year Book 2.* Cambridge: Cambridge University Press.

Kohli, R. 1972 *Hindi ke Vishesan Pratyayõ kaa bhaashaavaigyaanik adhyayan.* Delhi: M.A. dissertation.

Koul, O. N. 1981. ed. *Topics in Hindi Linguistics,* Vol 2. New Delhi: Bahri Publications.

Kuyrlowich, J. 1960. Hindi Accentuation as a Historical Problem. In Krishnamurti, Bh. ed. *Studies in Indian Languages.* Poona: Deccan, College, 208-211.

Lakoff, G. 1970. *Irregularity in Syntax.* New York: Holt, Rinehart & Winston

Lees, R. 1960. *The Grammar of English Nominalizations.* The Hague: Mouton.

Leiber, R. 1981. *On the Organization of the Lexicon.* Bloomington: Indiana University Linguistic Club.

Maheshchandra. 1978. *Parinishthita Hindi Ka Rupgramika Adhyayana.* Meerut: Kalpana Prakashan.

Marchand, H. 1969. *The Categories and Types of Present day English Word-Formation.* Munich: C.H. Beck Verlagasbuchandlung.

Martinet, A. 1964. *Elements of General Linguistics.* London: Faber.

Martohardjono, G. 1986. *Morphology and External Evidence: A Study of the Ford and Singh Model of the Lexicon.* Montreal, M.A. thesis.

Martohardjono, G. and Singh, R. 1992. Integral Listing and Speech Errors. *Linguistische Berichte* 139: 153-68.

Matthews, P. H. 1972. *Inflectional Morphology: A Theoretical Study Based on Aspects of Latin Verb Conjugation.* Cambridge: Cambridge University Press.

_______. 1974. *Morphology: An Introduction to the Theory of Word-Structure.* Cambridge: Cambridge University Press.

Matilal, B.K. 1985. *Logic, Language and Reality.* Delhi: Motilal Banarsidass.

Mey, J. 1685. *Whose language*? Amsterdam: John Benjamin.

Mohanan, K.P. 1982. *Lexical Phonology.* MIT: Ph.D. Thesis.

_________. 1986. *The Theory of Lexical Phonology.* Dordrecht: Foris.

Nespital, H. 1990. On the Relation of Hindi to its Regional Dialects. In Offredi, M. *Language versus Dialect: Linguistic and Literary Essays in Hindi, Tamil and Sarnami.* Delhi: Munshiram Manoharlal, 3-24.

Nida, E. 1949. *Morphology: The Descriptive Analysis of Words.* Ann Arbor: University of Michigan Press.

Ohala, M. 1972. *Topics in Hindi-Urdu Phonology.* California: Ph.D Thesis.

______. 1983. *Aspects of Hindi Phonology.* Delhi: Motilal Banarasidass.

———. 1985. Aspects of Phonology Revisited. *Indian Linguistics* 46:13-20.

———. 1987. Schwa Deletion in Hindi by linear and non-linear routes. Paper presented at the *XIV International Congress of Linguistics.* Berlin.

Pandey, P.K. 1990. Hindi Schwa Deletion. *Lingua* 82:272-311.

Pesetsky, D. 1985. Morphology and Logical Form. *Linguistic Inquiry* 16:196-246.

Phillips, B. S. and Bouma, L. 1980. The Acquisition of German Plurals in Native Children and Non-Native Adults. In Nehls, D. ed. *Studies in Language Acquisition.* Heidelberg.

Platts, J. T. 1873(first pub. 1941) first Indian edition 1967. *A Grammar of the Hindustani or Urdu Language.* Delhi: Munshiram Manoharlal.

Pray, B.R. 1970. *Topics in Hindi-Urdu Grammar.* Berkeley: Centre for South and South Asia Studies.

Rai, A. 1984. *A House Divided : The Origin and Development of Hindi/ Hindavi.* Delhi: Oxford University Press.

Rajgopalan, N.V. 1973. *Hindi ka Bhashavaigyanika Vyakarana.* Agra: Kendriya Hindi Sansthan.

Randall, J.H. 1982. *Morphological Structure and Language Acquisition.* Amherst, Mass.; Graduate Linguistic Students Association.

_______. 1987. Inheritance. In Wilkens, ed. *Thematic Relations.* New York.

Roeper, T. 1987. *The Syntax of Compound Reference.* Amherst University of Mass.

Robitaille, R. 1986. *Le Role de la Morphologie Processus de Reconaissance Lexical.* Montreal, M.A Thesis.

Sapir, E. 1921. *Language.* New York: Hartcourt Brace & World.

Schultz, Rev. B. 1744. *Grammatica Hindostanica.* Callenberg: Halle Saxonum.

Selkirk, E.O. 1982. *The Syntax of Words.* Cambridge, Mass.: MIT Press .

Shapiro, M.C. 1976. The Analysis of Hindi Morphologically Related Verb Sets. *Indian Linguistics* 37.1:1-44.

Sharma, A. 1958. *A Basic Grammar of Modern Hindi.* (2nd ed.) New Delhi: Central Hindi Directorate.

Shivprasad, R. 1875. *Hindi Vyakaraṇa.* Allahabad: The Government Press.

Shrilal, P. 1855. *Bhasha-Candrodaya.* Agra.

Siegal, D. 1979. *Topics in English Morphology.* New York: Garland.

Singh, A. 1994. *The Phonology Morphology Interface : A case from Hindi.* Delhi, Ph. D. Thesis.

Singh, A.B. 1965. Hindi Verbs: An Outline. *Indian Linguistics* 26:154-171.

Singh, J.D. 1971. Hindi Verb Conjugation. *Indian Linguistics* 32.2:91-90.

_______. 1973. The Representation of Hindi Grammatical Categories. *Indian Linguistics* 34.2:120-133.

Singh, K.S. 1978. ed. *Readings in Hindi-Urdu Linguistics.* New Delhi: National Publishing House.

_____ 1987. Well-formedness Conditions and Phonological Theory. In Dressler, W.U. et al. ed. *Phonologica 1984* (London 1987) 273-85.

Singh, R. and Martohardjono, G. 1988. Intermorphology and Morphological Theory: A Plea for a Concession. In Flynn, S. and O'Neil, W. eds. *Linguistic Theory and Second Language Acquisition.* Dorderecht: Kluwer, 362-82.

Singh, R. 1982. Some Redundant Compounds in Morden Hindi. *Lingua* 56:345-351.

_____. 1987. Well-formedness Conditions and Phonological Theory. In Dressler, W.U. ed. *Phonologica 1984* (Cambridge 1987) 273-285.

_____. 1990. Do we Really Want a Syntax Organ? *Indian Linguistics* 49: 109-115.

_______. 1991 Iterference and Contemporary Phonological Theory. *Language Learning* 41.2:157-75.

______. 1992. Two Morphological Notes: A Sharp and a Flat. *Revue Quebecoise de Linguistique* 21.2: 183-91.

______. 1995. Natural Phono(morpho)logy: a view from the outside. In Hurch, B. and Rhodes, R. eds. *Natural phonology: The State of the Art.* Berlin 1-38.

Singh, R. and Ford, A. 1980. Flexion, Dérivative et Panini. In Koernet, E. F .K. ed. *Studies on the Theory and History of Linguistic Science* 20. Amsterdam, 323-332.

Sommerstein, A. H. 1977. *Modern Phonology.* London: Edward Arnold.

Sproat, R. 1985. On Deriving the Lexicon. *The Linguistic Review* 5:185-96.

Srivastava, R.N., 1968. Theory of Morphophonematics of Aspirated Phonemes of Hindi. *Acta Linguistica* 363-73.

______. 1970. How Empty is the Abstract Verb (+cause): A Case Grammar of Hindi Causal-Verb Morphology. In Ghatage, A.M. et al eds. *Proceedings of the First All India Conference of Linguistics.* Poona: Linguistic Society of India. 61-76.

_______.1974. Review of D.D.Sharma's. *Syllabic Structure of Hindi and Panjabi* (Chandigarh: Punjab University Publication Bureau 1971). *Indian Linguistics* 35:70-79.

————. 1987. Hindi mẽ Naskiya, Anusvar aur Anunasikta ki Samasya. In Tewari, B.N. ed. *Hindi Bhasha ki Dhavani-sanracna.* Delhi: Sahitya Sahkar 100-108.

________. 1976. Shabd: Ek Saidhantik Vivechan. *Gveshṇa*: 47-69.

Singh, S. 1976. *Morphonemics in Contemporary Hindi.* Lucknow: Ph.D. Thesis.

Tiersma, P.M. 1982. Local and General Markedness. *Language* 58.4:832 848.

______. 1990. *Shabd: Adhyayan aur Samsyaayẽ.*" Agra.

Upreti, M.L. 1964. *Hindi mẽ Pratyay Vichar.* Agra: Vinod Pustak Mandir.

Urciuoli, B. 1991. The Political Topography of Spanish and English: The View from a New York Puertirican Neighborhood. *American Ethnologist.* Rpt. in Singh, R. ed. *Towards a Critical Sociolinguistics.* Amsterdam: Benjamin

Vajpeyi, K. 1958. *Hindi Shabdanushasan.* Kashi: Nagri Pracharni Sabha.

van Olphen, H. 1975. Aspects of Tense and Mood in the Hindi Verb. *Indo-Iranian Journal* 16.4:284-301.

Vennemann, T. 1974. Words and Syllables in Natural Generative Grammar. In Bruck, A. et al eds. *CLS Parasession on Natural Phonology.* Chicago: Chicago Linguistic Society, 346-374.

Verma, M.K. 1971. *The Structure of Noun Phrase in English and Hindi.* Delhi: Motilal Banarsidass.

Verma, S. 1961. *Critical Studies in the Phonetic Observations of Indian Grammarians.* Delhi: Munshiram Manoharlal.

Vidyalankar, J. 1970. Hindi mẽ Lingaanushasan, *Gaveshaṇa* 8.16: 48-66.

Vinson, J. 1899. *Manual de la Langue Hindoustani* (*Urdu et Hindi*) *Grammaire, Texts, Vocabularies.* Paris: J. Maisonn Euve.

William, E. 1981. Argument Structure and Morphology. *The Linguistic Review* 1:81-114.

Williams, M. 1858a. *An Easy Introduction to the Study of Hindustani, in which the English alphabet is adopted to the expression of Hindustani Words with a full syntax.* London: Longman.

_____ 1858b. *Rudiments of Hindustani Grammar.* London: Cheltenham.

Wurzel, W.U. 1970. *Studien Zür Deutshen Lautstruktur.* Berlin.

AUTHOR INDEX